THE LONG GREEN TUNNEL

What They're Saying:

David Barol's account of his amazing journey is packed with humorous and astute observations about the Appalachian Trail and the wonders of this beautiful planet. If you liked Bill Bryson's A Walk in the Woods, *you'll love David's prose!*
— Ben Feldman, Author

I thoroughly enjoyed this Trip along "Your Trail."
— Marcia Hineline, Park Ranger

. . . brings the humor of the Catskills to the gritty reality of the Appalachian Trail
— Leah Hoffman, Anthropologist

The Long Green Tunnel *makes me better appreciate the generation who worked so hard to make this a high-integrity, productive nation.*
— Andrea Trulson Dolph, Author

Read the book in two days on the beach. Loved it.
— Mark Booz, Attorney

This is an extremely engaging account of a young man's adventures on the Appalachian Trail in a time that seems long ago (the mid-1970s). The real focus of the book, though, isn't the trials, tribulations, and rewards of hiking the AT, but on the impact the hike had on a friendship. It's also a story of what happens when we try to follow someone else's dreams rather than our own. The obvious starting point for comparison is Bill Bryson's A Walk in the Woods, *but I not only enjoyed* The Long Green Tunnel *more,*

I think it's better written. And there were lots of places where I laughed out loud. I'm looking forward to volume 2.
— Scott Nance, International Attorney

I thoroughly enjoyed reading The Long Green Tunnel. *I couldn't wait to share it with someone so I gave my first copy to a friend. I'm scheduled to receive 3 more copies; 2 for friends and another to replace the one I gave away. I'm already looking forward to the sequel(s).*
— David Kirkwood

An enjoyable read about the author as a young man who follows someone else's dream. The book has thoughtful elements that reminded me of Zen and the Art of Motorcycle Maintenance, *in its consideration of quality, although the story is much lighter, betraying a youthful playfulness in the author simultaneously serious and lighthearted like jazz.*
— Intellectual Wanderer

I loved the author's descriptions of the neighborhood he grew up in Philadelphia and the volatile time in our history during the 60s and 70s. His descriptions of blacks and whites getting along during this time and his descriptions of his father's influence over him and his integrated neighborhood are real life and true. The authors' love of books is obvious as he reads his way along his trip down the trail and his language skills paint a beautiful picture of what it is like hiking so many miles. Lots of fun and look forward to the next installment of this journey!
— Marvin Resnick, Real Estate Developer

For information about permission to reproduce
selections from this book, write to:

Permissions, Bala House Publishing
Info@BalaHousePublishing.com

For information about special discounts for bulk
purchases, please contact: .

Bala House Special Sales at
Info@BalaHousePublishing.com

Manufacturing by CreateSpace.

Cover art by Jada Byrd.
Illustrations by Jada Byrd, Galen McMullen, Morgan McMullen,
Chris Murphy, and Jasmina Raknic.

Book design by Josef Beery.

Library of Congress Cataloging-in-Publication Data
Barol, David 1957-
Notes From The Trail: The Long Green Tunnel / David Barol.

ISBN 978-0-9914559-0-4

NOTES FROM THE TRAIL
BOOK ONE

The Long Green Tunnel

David Barol

Bala House Publishing
Bala Cynwyd, Pennsylvania

CONTENTS

ILLUSTRATIONS

To my little buddy, who has begun his own journey through life, I dedicate this book.
You were my muse in writing this.

Also, to my dad:
"So I'll meet 'im later on, in the place where 'e is gone . . ."

WARNING!!

Do not pick up this book if you want to read something on hiking. This is not the book for you. Put — the Kindle — back.

This is no more a book on hiking than *Huckleberry Finn* was a book on boating. Sure, Huck Finn had something to do with a river — but that is not the point.

Notes from the Trail starts with the promise of great adventure. After flying to Maine, two young men reached Mt. Katahdin to begin their journey south along the Appalachian Trail. Okay, so far it sounds like hiking.

As an aside, now more than 3,000 people annually attempt to hike the entire Appalachian Trail, either from south to north or from north to south. Walking twenty miles a day, every day, just for a week, sounds exhausting. Extending that pace to one hundred straight days still won't get you to the other end. Who in their right mind would want to do such a thing?

Each person who begins such a quest — and this includes all the other journeys such as the Pacific Crest Trail or El Camino de Santiago in Spain — soon realizes the challenge is not the length they must walk or the heights they must climb. Rather, it is the journey they must take in their own mind. Many who start soon learn that the journey is not so much physical as it is metaphysical. Three quarters of those who begin the Appalachian Trail stop before the end, many limping away in pain, some running out of time, but there are others who find what they came for, having reached the destination that matters most.

This book touches a bit on adventure and blisters, vistas and mud, but it explores so much more than a trail. It explores a young man's journey in search of his dream. For without his dream to guide him, he wandered into a five-month walk in the woods aimlessly following the dream of his friend.

Who knew hiking partners would go through the same ups and downs as married couples? We fall in love with the idea of a future together but we fear ruining the courtship by digging beneath the surface. Just so we are clear: this is no more a book on relationships than it is a book about hiking, but what goes on between these two young men shapes the story.

This trip will forever mark these two young men. There are defining moments for all of us that measure how we grow from one stage of our lives to another. For my father, one such moment came while visiting his aunt on a Sunday in December, 1941. My first such moment came when I was six, looking at the news from Dallas. The picture I remember most is the fallen President's little boy saluting the funeral procession. As I got older, I remember watching the national draft on television, lotteries from which nobody emerged a winner.

I can tell you where I was when I heard the first footsteps on the moon; I even looked up. And I remember my eighteenth birthday, when the news showed those frantic people scrambling to board the last helicopter leaving the roof of the US Embassy in Saigon before the Viet Cong entered the compound and brought the Viet Nam war to a close.

That era shaped me, but mine are the eyes of a generational in-betweener. The requirement to register for the draft ended a month before it was my turn. We were the younger siblings: too young to fight in Viet Nam, march on Washington, or get down at Woodstock. We saw the body counts, bra burnings, and sexual revolution on the news, but we most likely did so because we had turned on the television early so as not to miss the beginning of *Gilligan's Island*.

I fall between the Viet Nam generation and those younger, for whom Viet Nam and the Sixties were historical events, for whom the chase of the White Bronco means something but the connection between Roosevelt Grier and Bobby Kennedy, not so much.

I grew up amongst so much change I thought change was normal. I lived in the fourth largest city in America and attended public schools. I was a white kid in a school district that turned increasingly integrated with each passing year. I witnessed the turmoil caused by the frustration of segregation, the murder of Martin Luther King, and with the mutual distrust of the police. The dynamics that played out colored my impressions of people and influenced what I consider important.

Although the Sixties affected me, and the city influenced me, my parents raised me. They believed in the power of a community action to change lives and they viewed the community as the foundation of the great nation we could be, a nation in which all its people embodied the sacred ideals on which it was founded. My parents worked with passion to keep our neighborhood from disintegrating like so many others. They did not turn and run, but rather they greeted newcomers with an outstretched hand and integrated them into their lives.

My father's search for meaning led him to the words expressed most elegantly by our third president, Thomas Jefferson. During a summer trip, he and my mother visited the University of Virginia where they signed me up for an admissions packet. Both the university Jefferson created, and the man himself, influenced me and, in turn, this book.

You can see already that *The Long Green Tunnel*, the first book in the **Notes From The Trail** series, is not a book about how to rub two sticks together. It searches for dreams, both that of the books' storyteller, and for the rest of us, the American Dream.

I am not saying that stories about flies, swamps, and mountain ledges are not important. Perhaps these were the challenges this young man needed to head him in the right direction. If, despite all the warnings, you still want a book on hiking, you will find some rocks to climb and tents to pitch inside. And, did you hear the one about the moose?

Let me be perfectly clear about the time and place. The book starts in Maine in 1977. The storyteller keeps a journal, writing about what took place each day. The present takes place as he is writing. What took place ten minutes earlier was the past and what he anticipated eating in a few minutes is the future — even though that too happened a long time ago, when our country still had a king, when we were briefly fighting no wars, and when our President addressed the nation looking like Mr. Rogers.

That's a bit about what you have in store. It is a journey. It takes place along a trail. But it definitely is not a book about hiking.

— DAVID BAROL

CHAPTER ONE

Optîmîsm

JUNE 1, AM

Abol Campground, Baxter State Park

We left Philadelphia yesterday at 7:37 aboard a Boeing 737. After switching planes in Boston, we arrived in Bangor, Maine. It was my first flight and my first holding pattern. In two and a half hours we travelled 700 miles; in the next four, we travelled ten. I learned already that flying beats hitchhiking.

When I made the plane reservations, the ticket agent asked, "Shall I book a return ticket?"

"Nah, don't bother," I said, "I'll walk back."

I guess she did not get many calls from Appalachian Trail hikers, although I am not an official one yet. I won't earn that distinction until later today.

What joy it will be to hike every day under these blue New England skies and the bright but not overly warm sun. In a few minutes, Rand, my hiking partner and I will leave our campsite to climb Mount Katahdin, the highest mountain in Maine. We could see Katahdin from fifty miles away, looming large and solitary against the sky. Tomorrow we will begin our journey south to Georgia, although Katahdin will continue to loom over our shoulders for days to come.

I am here because Rand asked me. We have been great friends since the first day of college, at the University of Virginia. It was an honor to be the one person he wanted to go with on this great adventure. We are so alike. Both Eagle Scouts, we get the job done without having to be asked and we both desire to get the job done right. We are a hand and a glove, a pair of bookends, a hot dog and a bun — perfectly matched and identically suited to hike the Appalachian Trail.

JUNE 1, PM

Katahdin Stream Campground

Now, then; that wasn't so bad. Yeah, right.

It took us nine hours to climb Katahdin in what has been the most exhausting day of my life. Fortunately, the ranger drove our packs from last night's campground to this one, so we did not have to carry them up and over that beast.

We started the day walking on a path that began to rise and fall but never falling as much as it rose. Within minutes, Rand and I stood mesmerized by an amazing sight: a blowdown where hundreds of trees leaned one against the other. From where we stood, we could see an entire valley of green trees surrounding a huge swath of grey dying wood and barren soil.

Rand asked me to help him pursue his lifelong dream of hiking the Appalachian Trail. Intelligent and introspective, I never once heard him say an unkind word to anyone.

That was before today.

As we stared in awe at the blowdown, he said something that left me speechless. I would rather not write it down as I hope to shake it off. I know if I dwell on it, I will make it worse. Like water on a duck's back, I will let this drip off, besides, it was the only cloud on an otherwise sunny day.

After saying his piece, he abruptly left. I hiked alone for the next hour. When I broke through the treeline I could see the horizon far to the east. I nearly caught up with Rand as we scrambled up a field of rocks. Ahead, I saw the top of the mountain and the beginning of the AT. I pressed on without pause. Pulling myself onto what I thought was the top of the mountain, I gaped at what looked like another mountain left to climb.

I had reached the summit, not the peak. I walked on, passing a sign that read "Thoreau's Spring," but there was no water, which may explain why Thoreau went crazy hiking in Maine. Henry David Thoreau travelled this way more than a century ago, then wrote about it. I will try to write about Maine while holding on to my sanity.

In a mile I reached Baxter Peak, where I touched the sign that marked the start of the Appalachian Trail, making me official. I turned south and, from then on, walked on the Appalachian Trail, the 2,100 mile footpath that will take me from Maine to Springer Mountain. I became a Southbounder, not to be confused with those other Thruhikers known as Northbounders, who will invade these woods in a few weeks after their migration north from Georgia.

Climbing Katahdin was hard; climbing down was treacherous. I lowered myself from one granite ledge to another. Looking left or looking right made no difference: looking in either direction meant looking straight down. Holding onto one ledge to drop to another gave me the sense that I was one slip from falling. I inched out from one ledge and then dropped to the ledge below, fighting the image that I could easily bounce off a rock and fall over the side. From looking out from such heights, I could see how someone thought up infinity.

I heard about people who became so frightened they stuck to their ledge, not budging until other hikers guided them down. One such rescuer helping an older gentleman, slipped, and broke his own leg.

Rand and I descended without incident and found our packs at the ranger station. We slept under the stars in an empty campsite. Tomorrow, it all begins.

Hurd Lean-to

Unlike the blue sky of yesterday, today it rained off and on. Both my feet felt as if I dropped them into a creek, which, in fact, I did. After that misadventure, I changed the dressings on my feet, put on dry socks, and continued walking. But the wet bushes, the dripping trees, and the muddy trail soaked my shoes so within minutes both feet were sloshing wet once again.

At the end of the day, when I arrived at the Hurd Lean-to, I was greeted by a chorus of "Welcome, Thruhiker!"

I walked my first complete day on the Appalachian Trail, having touched the marker on top of Mt. Katahdin yesterday. I am a Thruhiker. Next stop: Springer Mountain.

A lean-to is a small building with three sides and a sloped roof. Although Hurd Lean-to must be twenty feet across, it feels crowded. My partner was the fourth to arrive and I made number five. Three more came from the south, having walked all week. The two who greeted me hail from Texas.

They hiked north from Monson, Maine, with the hope of climbing Katahdin. After that they will hitchhike to New Hampshire for a week in the White Mountains; it will take us a month to walk there.

The other guy who arrived before me hoped to climb Katahdin today, but the rangers closed the mountain because of the rain. What a difference one day makes. Rather than risk waiting endlessly at the base of the mountain, he began his hike towards Georgia, figuring he could come back to climb Katahdin some other year. It seems a shame to miss the start of the Trail after going through so much effort just to reach the base of the great mountain.

He is a tall, thin guy with sandy hair and a tiny blue pack. I cannot imagine he has much in the way of food in there. He pitched his blue one-man tent away from the lean-to and stayed by himself. Not having climbed Katahdin disqualifies him as an official Thruhiker so he can keep his distance.

The Texas guys are well-seasoned hikers who use many of the skills they learned in Viet Nam. They pack light and carry cooked rice which they eat hot or cold. They told us not to salt our food because salt is "bad for your health"; instead they carried miso paste, the fermented soybean concentrate that has "a tenth the sodium of salt." We carry salt tablets with us in case of dehydration and yet these two told us we eat too much salt.

I read books on hiking, most notably the one written by Colin Fletcher, the Patron Saint of backpackers. My partner, Rand, and I are both Eagle Scouts, so we know our way around a backpack. We planned and organized everything perfectly. After all this work, my head is so full that one more suggestion would cause it to burst.

❧ ❧ ❧

I moved away from the lean-to to keep writing as those two make me feel deflated. They just warned that we "are in for a week of mud and mosquitoes; you don't know what you've got yourselves in for." Then they told me my pack is too heavy; I will not need all the clothing I packed, and I will never have time to read the half dozen books I carry with me.

Well, at least I climbed Katahdin.

Today, there were plenty of chances to read. I walked a total of ten miles, all by myself, and although I am tired, it did not take much time. It rained most of the day but I enjoyed the few breaks when the sun broke through the overcast sky. I found a log or rock to sit upon or a tree to lean against so I could continue to read *"One Flew over the Cuckoo's Nest"* by Ken Kesey. I am so into the book I can pick up the story no matter where I left off. Although, I am not sure where Kesey is coming from, whether he wants to expose the conditions in mental hospitals or wants to point out the abuse of the insanity plea, he sure knows how to tell a good story. I feel enclosed in the mental ward as I read this book even though I am reading it in a forest without walls.

The trail south of Katahdin wound through a dense thicket of trees along brooks and streams. There were no scenic overlooks, just a never ending wood. For most of the walk, I could not see the sky as the trees on either side of the path met just above my head. I saw no views but instead walked inside a long, green tunnel.

I crossed a road at the southern edge of Baxter State Park, which the guidebook declared was the last hard paved road before entering the "100 Mile Wilderness," a Tolkien name if ever there was one. Although I left first, my hiking partner passed me and remained out of sight for the rest of the day. Since there was no one to share my thoughts or observations with, I read. Not a problem, really as I am an unrepentant Marxist. It was Groucho who said, "Outside of a dog, a book is man's best friend; inside a dog, it's too dark to read."

I thought of a thousand different ideas as I walked, but like a night's dreams, I can barely remember any of them. So I decided to jot my thoughts on a paper whenever I pause so I can transfer them to these pages each night. So, if I do go insane like Thoreau, my biographers — or psychoanalysts — can mark the exact moment.

JUNE 3

Rainbow Stream Lean-to

Here we are at the Rainbow Stream Laundromat. That is how it looks with all the multi-colored shirts, towels, and socks hanging from the rafters. The sky is grey and the air cold but after two days of it, I expect no more rain.

The lean-to overlooks a stream with water just warm enough to soak my blistered feet. The blisters are not healing because my feet are wet all the time.

Nevertheless, I found my pace today. There is no greater joy than to roll along, uphill and down. Despite the rolling pace, the hiker should refrain from becoming too ecstatic about his good days for then it follows he will become overwhelmed by the bad. A bad week in Maine and we will find our lonely hiker standing along the highway holding a sign that reads: "Home." Separate the emotion from the walking

— that's what I say — take it all in stride. Walking should be the means to see beauty; for if you are into the beauty of walking, then you run the risk of being overwhelmed by the ugliness as well.

Rand and I have our own approach to hiking together. We don't. In fact, we never hike within one hundred yards of each other: far enough for each hiker to feel alone; far enough for swinging branches to come to rest; for red packs to disappear; for mother ruffed grouses to become unruffled. Still it seems strange to hike the Trail with someone and not see him.

I guess I will get used to it.

JUNE 4

Nahmakanta Lake Lean-to

I am sitting by the tent waiting for Rand to focus his camera in the setting light. In a few moments, the quiet guy from Michigan will take a picture of us pretending to study a map. I have now spent three nights with this guy but have exchanged a total of ten words. He set up his tent in the woods, far from ours, and kept to himself. He will leave after the picture but we will share a campsite with him again tonight at a spot some twelve miles away.

There were two good reasons why we pitched a tent by a lean-to. The first was that the lean-to lacked a platform and the mud floor looked like a pig sty. The second was that at every turn, we were enveloped by clouds of buzzing insects — black flies and mosquitoes — forcing us to spend our time zipped inside our tent. The flies were tiny little black things, not much bigger than gnats. They swarmed but did not land.

The mosquitoes showed no such inhibitions. They landed at will and my face has the welts to prove it.

My tale of woe does not end with my face. I got blisters within an hour of landing in Maine. I am like a soldier just landed in Saigon who gets hit crossing the tarmac by a jeep. I got my blisters trying to thumb a ride one hundred miles south of Kathadin.

Each morning, I wash the blisters with Dr. Bronner's Peppermint Soap to get the dirt out. After the foot has dried, I apply an antibacterial ointment, next, a Band-Aid, followed by moleskin, all of which I wrap with adhesive tape. The moleskin reduces the friction between the tender spots and the boot, thus making it possible to walk without crippling pain. I still feel pain, especially when I start in the morning, but it is not crippling. I told Rand that with the blister, the heavy pack, and the rough terrain, I have found it difficult to find my pace. "I can cope with two out of the three," I said, "but not all three at once." And so I delude myself.

I carry my healing supplies in a small bag in the lower left pocket of my pack. The clever people who designed my pack built it into two sections, with multiple pockets, so I do not have to rummage to reach stuff. I store items of a similar function in nylon bags. If I need my flashlight, I can touch my pack, move my hand to the top right pocket, find the zipper and reach in. Matches are in the same pocket, with the rest of my emergency gear like my compass and whistle. My poncho always gets rolled and stored in the bottom section of the pack, so even if I have the rain cover on, all I have to do is uncover the bottom section and pull it out. A place for everything and everything in its place.

This morning, about two miles into the hike, I reached the Pollywog Stream Ford. A "ford" is just another name for "there is no bridge." Pollywog is a wide stream with a fast current, filled with water that was melting snow only a few moments before.

Rather than ruin my first aid by walking across the stream, I came up with a solution worthy of Thomas Jefferson. My partner and I met at the University of Virginia, Mr. Jefferson's University, which remains a living museum to the ingenuity, the love of learning and design, and to the civility of this great man. He filled his home at Monticello with his clever ideas, not unlike my backpack.

I carried the plastic trash bag the ranger gave us in Baxter State Park with the warning, "You packed it in; you can pack it out." I stuck my bandaged foot into the bag and pulled the drawstrings taut. I next wrapped my nylon rain chaps around the top of the bag forming an airtight seal. Then I carefully stepped across the stream. What a sight I must have been. With a giant pack on my back, two boots in one hand, I stepped gingerly across the bone-chilling creek with my other hand clutching the drawstring of — a — bag — filled — with water.

I have so let Jefferson down.

This hike is about more than trees and mountains. I am walking a trail that winds through the pathways of my mind. I am going to make a habit of writing something each day without fail.

JUNE 6

The Old Logging Camp

Yesterday started innocently enough with the three of us planning to meet at the "Old Logging Camp," which the guidebook placed twelve miles south of where we started and 1.7 miles past the "Old Stag Antlers Camp." The quiet guy left first while Rand walked to the lake to supplement the two brook trout a fisherman gave us, using the hook and line he packed. He came up short but sautéed the two trout on the Svea stove.

After eating our pack food for three days, I relished every bite of these fish that lived their lives in Nahmakanta Lake. The water was clear, cold, and inviting; the only way to get there was by walking the Appalachian Trail or taking the gravel jeep road through lands owned by the Great Northern Paper Company. You can taste the fresh mountain lake with every bite.

As I was eating, a friendly — although odd smelling — Malamute padded over. I gave the dog's cheeks a shake then looked at my hands. He had been sniffing at our privy, which was nothing more than a branch nailed across two stumps.

"Let's go boy," I said.

I washed my hands in the lake, which deserved better. Stopping by the truck of the fishermen who gave us the trout, I ordered the dog to stay. When I returned to the site there he was to greet me, wagging his tail.

It started to rain so Rand went back into the tent to read while I took off, walking the first five miles along the gravel road. The guidebook called this stretch the "100 Mile Wilderness." There are some roads made of gravel and some just of mud, but for the most part, we hike along dirt paths cut through forests. And, falling upon whatever surface we have walked, has been the rain that has accompanied us since we left Katahdin.

I did not invite the dog along, but along he came. Instead of following me, he led me, with his tongue lolling to the side. He stayed fifty feet in front occasionally looking back to make sure I was still there. I yelled for him to go home but each time I did, he would run further ahead. His fur was black and white but his eyes were as blue as the sky, not the sky I could see in Maine, but somewhere. He was solidly built with a full coat of fur and obviously had been well-cared for.

For two hours he trotted in front of me, occasionally falling behind to follow a scent, but always racing ahead. Strange, but this has been the closest I have come to actually hiking with someone since entering Maine.

How great it would be to hike the Trail with a dog like him. He was so full of spirit he almost danced when he ran. I imagined him sitting next to me by the campfire and curling against me at night, adding an extra body's heat for these cold, rainy nights. A malamute is a dog born to pull a sled, which explains why he felt it necessary to run in front of me, looking back, laughing to himself about how he anointed himself the lead dog. I guess I helped him self-actualize.

After two hours of brisk walking, I saw the double blazes signaling a change of direction. The Trail left the gravel road and cut into the woods. I stopped. The dog kept walking but when he turned to look for me, I ran toward him. He sprung in the air and raced as fast as he could. When I reached the turnoff, I lunged into the high grass and crawled behind a tree. A few moments later, he galloped past, thinking I playfully ran the five miles back to the lake.

I felt bad for tricking him but hoped Rand would think to do the same. This was the most beautiful dog in the world but he belonged to somebody and I could not take such a magnificent animal. If I allowed him to follow me that would be tantamount to stealing and, if I put myself into his owner's boots, I could not imagine losing such a great dog.

Anyone setting out on such an adventure needs to decide upon a moral code and then realize that circumstances will test that resolution. During our first week at Virginia, we signed pledges to support the student run Honor System, which tolerates neither lying, cheating, nor stealing. After high school, where there had been plenty of lying, cheating, and stealing, I found it refreshing to go through college knowing that the teachers compared my best efforts with the best efforts of others, without the fear of falling behind those who were getting ahead by cheating.

My partner and I shared a house with ten other guys. None of us had locks on our doors. Although I did not have much worth stealing, I never had so much as a pencil taken from me. But we are many miles away from The University and its Honor System. Can we now lie, cheat and steal? Does what happens on the Trail, stay on the Trail?

I would never take another person's dog, Honor System or no Honor System. Maybe he belonged to the fishermen but not finding them by their truck figured they had abandoned him; all the while they were sitting in their boat in the middle of the lake. Conversely, what if someone drove into the back country, let him out, and then drove off hoping to save on dog food bills. In that case, sticking with us might be his only way to survive. I may have left a domesticated dog to die because of my over developed concern over honor. I can hear my father's warning, "Justice tempered with mercy."

After pulling a fast one on the malamute, I entered a grove of saplings. I kept thinking about the dog, hoping I did the right thing. At least if he did not belong to the fishermen, they would realize that the dog's fate lay with them and they could drive him to safety.

After an hour, I reached the Potaywadjo Lean-to. I figured my partner would reach me any minute; he walked so much faster and he did not have blisters. According to the guidebook, the spring by the lean-to is the "largest and coldest in all Maine" and is "A joy to the hiker." They were not kidding:

the water tasted sweet and cold. Bubbles gurgled from the white sandy bottom just as they would from a water cooler. After drinking my fill, I moved on; the mosquitoes were thirstier than I.

Three miles farther, I came upon the ruins of the Old Antler's Camp on the Lower Jo-Mary Lake. I could stop just for a moment to look at the abandoned buildings; the mosquitoes drove me on. This camp, and many more like it, flourished for years as hunting and fishing camps in the Maine Woods. You could fly to these camps by seaplane as they all sit on the shores of clear pristine lakes. But for the most part, the camps have disappeared, decaying into the wilderness. In fact, it seems that most of Maine has returned to its primordial state. I have walked along stone walls holding back trees and mud from meeting other trees and mud. Maine is one of the few places with fewer people on the land today than the century before.

Judging from the guidebook, I was still two miles from the "Old Logging Camp." I figured that when I reached the camp, I would join the quiet hiker in his blue tent to avoid the mosquitoes. Maybe there would be some old cabins or a dining hall, something to mark the spot.

I was getting weary. The mosquitoes ignored the rain and forced me to keep moving, blanketing my hands and face whenever I stopped. I smeared my face with Old Woodsman bug repellent — scented with that distinctive smell of tar — ignoring the price I would one day pay with brain damage.

I moved on, surprised my partner had not reached me. On the other days, although I left first, he passed me within the first few hours. I would hear his footsteps and sense him walking behind me. I would quicken my pace but he would continue to gain on me. Then, if the path widened or my step faltered, he would pass me and keep going without a word or a wave.

I kept walking, occasionally stopping to look at the map. I saw neither the blue tent nor anything that resembled an old logging camp. And yet, given the time since my last landmark, I should easily have travelled the distance. The trouble was, I did not know what a new logging camp looked like, let alone an old logging camp.

I crossed the mouth of Mud Pond on a series of submerged logs and then inched along a birch sapling that someone laid from one bank to the other of a nearby stream. It wobbled up and down so fast I would have fallen into the rushing water had I not jumped back to shore. Perplexed, I looked upstream for a crossing. I crossed several streams in Maine — few with bridges. This would not normally pose a challenge but with all the rain, the water funneling through the banks made the crossing dangerous. Twenty yards upstream, I could see how I might hop from rock to rock. As usual, I slipped and fell in.

At least I was not getting any wetter. In the clearings, the drenching rain drove me on; in the woods, the droning mosquitoes kept me from stopping. It was raining too hard to read but I paused several times to give Rand the chance to catch up. The sky grew darker; I walked on.

I came upon a large fallen tree that blocked my path. I faced three choices. Either I could climb over it, or I could squeeze under it, or I could walk around it. Colin Fletcher in his *Complete Backpacker* advised us to walk around rather than step over and step over that which you cannot walk around — but never step on a fallen tree lest you slip.

I thought it strange that Rand had not passed me. I had already walked more miles than on any other day. I looked for either the old lumber camp or the blue tent of the silent hiker.

Then I came to the Great Northern Paper Company Road which crossed the Trail by Cooper Falls. I looked down at the yellow gravel brimming with water from the driving rain. From where I stood, I could not see the falls but after a day of walking in silence, the roar of the water jarred me. The old logging camp was two miles back, but I saw neither a blue tent nor any evidence of a camp of any sort. And where was Rand? It was hours and now fifteen miles since I last saw him; it was unlike him to lag behind.

A jeep passed; I waved. I read the wooden milepost: "14.5 miles north to Lake Nahmakanta Lean-to, 4 miles north to Jo-Mary Lake; 3.8 miles south to Cooper Falls Shelter. I pulled my watch out of my pack. It was quarter to six.

I felt the rising flame of panic. The three of us were supposed to camp over two miles back, but I could swear on the Bible, if I carried one, that nothing resembled a camp, let alone a camper. What if the silent hiker, in an effort to find dry ground, pitched his tent well off the Trail? Maybe I missed him. I did not know what to do, but figured walking south was pointless. If the silent hiker continued to the next lean-to that was his decision; my concern was with my partner.

Suppose something happened to him; suppose he slipped while stepping on a fallen tree and broke his leg; perhaps he had not read Colin Fletcher's book. Visions of death now surfaced in my mind. I saw him lying face down in a stream.

I saw myself lifting him up, his eyes bulging, his stiff arm pointing at me.

I needed to go back. I leaned my pack against a tree, put on my poncho, and reached into the "emergency pocket" to collect my whistle, pen knife, signal mirror, waterproof match case, and compass. I set off to find the others. But after a half-mile, I scolded myself for panicking — if I missed the lumber camp so maybe did the silent hiker, and Rand would certainly keep walking until he found me. I sat down on a log and tried to shake my head clear of panic, realizing I was in no condition to man a search. I overshot the mark by 2.3 miles, but what about the other hiker? Why did my partner not catch up? I returned to the gravel road.

I blew my whistle three times. Silence. Or rather, the incessant roar of the nearby falls and the constant pelting of the rain. I panicked once more. I knew I was alive; I had no recollection dying. And I figured I could continue the hike alone if need be. But what could have happened? How could my partner not have reached me? It was almost 6:30 and I was still alone. Rand does not take leisurely walks; he is a walking machine. Even when he spots me five miles, he passes me by noon.

I needed to calm my nerves, reduce my anxiety. I wished I could call my father. I did not know what to do and I needed to rely on someone with real experience. I put my poncho over my head and sought the calming influence of my book, *One Flew over the Cuckoo's Nest*, but my glasses kept fogging and the blue light that seeped through the poncho made reading difficult. "Enough of this," I said aloud. "I have to do something."

It was 6:45. I was hungry, tired, and thoroughly wet and cold. I knew I would weaken if I did not take care of myself and get out of the rain. I would have to make camp in the rain without the tent, the one piece of community equipment my partner carried.

What would Jefferson do? My poncho came with brass grommets at each corner and I carried a ground cloth. I packed one hundred feet of rope. Looking for a place to set up camp, I found a level piece of ground overlooking the falls. I tied a length of rope between two trees thinking I could lay my ground cloth over it and secure the four corners to the ground, sort of like a pup tent, but the mathematics let me down: a four by eight foot tarp, turned into an equilateral triangle has a base just two feet wide, not enough to shield a sleeping bag from the rain. It takes a lot more material to make a pup tent than I originally thought.

Again I asked, "What would Jefferson do?" I undid the rope and ran it through the two grommets at one end of my poncho. I then cut two more pieces of rope, running each from the remaining two corners to the bases of nearby trees. Instead of a pup tent, I created a lean-to, which covered an area four feet wide and about seven feet long, losing about a foot in length because of the thirty degree slope. It would keep me dry if I could solve two complications. Nothing kept the top of the poncho from bunching together and most lean-tos do not have a hole in the middle for a head to pop through.

The hood problem was easily remedied by pulling the draw strings taut. Only when I did so, I pulled so hard that I ripped the draw strings out of the lightweight nylon hood. The less destructive method for closing the hole then became clear: pull the hood through the hole so it would lie on top of the poncho in the direction of the flow of the rainwater.

Keeping the two corners from sliding together proved even less of a challenge. I pulled the two Kelty toggles — red, spring released — off the pack drawstrings and ran them through the top rope to hold the grommets in place. Next I slid the ground cloth and back pad under the poncho.

I kept my waterproof pack cover on my pack, which I propped against a tree. Not long after I finished, a pickup truck filled with lumberjacks stopped at the bridge. I walked down from my campsite thinking they might have news of the others but they walked past me to fill their beer cans from the stream. As nonchalantly as I could, I told them I was looking for two hikers, one of whom left ahead of me

and one behind, and asked if they heard of the "Old Logging Camp." One replied, "There's a lumber camp about a quarter mile down the Paper Road." "The *Old* logging camp," I said, "On the Appalachian Trail." He shrugged.

"You see, I don't know what to do. Should I stay here, go back and look for them, or keep walking?"

"You might as well stay here. You got your tent up already. Besides, you couldn't ask for a better view."

I ate some peanut butter on Logan Bread and read *Cuckoo's Nest,* in retrospect, maybe not the best book for someone on the brink of losing his sanity. I then ate another piece of Logan Bread. Darkness came and still my partner had not reached me. I was determined to rest, to get back my strength before I began searching. But was I avoiding my responsibility? If he's dead, he's dead; but what if he's not dead, what if he is two hours away from being dead and needs help now? I was shivering. I took my boots and wet socks off and slipped into my sleeping bag.

Maybe I could flag a passing jeep and get a ride to a telephone so I could call my dad; he would know what to do. My dad served in both WWII and Korea, with Officer Candidate School and law school jammed in between. Of course he is pretty old by now; he will turn fifty in October, but he is still reasonably sharp. He makes decisions all the time at work and at home; what decisions have I ever made? I needed his help. Should I go back, even if that means going all the way to Nahmakanta Lake, or should I sit here waiting for my partner to eventually show up? What if somehow he slipped by me and was waiting for me at the next lean-to? If that were the case and I went back, I would never find him; I would spend the rest of my life walking back and forth over the same fourteen point five miles while he sat with the silent hiker at the next lean-to.

Maybe Rand was testing me. On every day of this journey he passed me and then waited for me to show up to our destination. Maybe he zipped by me while I stooped to get water from the spring or maybe he deliberately failed to show to make me see what waiting feels like. I never purposefully finished late, and I think I walk fast, but he moves like a sled dog. I am an amateur walker to his professional hiker. I lay in the sleeping bag sucking on a tablespoon of peanut butter to warm my body. After a while, I fell asleep. All the while it rained.

Later, I can't tell how much, I awoke after hearing four whooping sounds. I sat up wondering "Could that be him?" The sounds were repeated. Maybe he is walking by, looking for me. It was pitch black out; I could not see a thing. "No. It couldn't be him," I reasoned as I lay my head back down, "the international distress signal is three, not four."

I awoke the next morning at first light, still alone. How could I have passed the blue tent? Did the silent hiker leave first? My father would know what to do. Maybe the new lumber camp would have a phone; I could call him from there. Maybe they would serve a hot breakfast. At the very least, I could see what a lumber camp looks like. I stuck a note on my pack and began walking in the direction the lumberjack had pointed. Where was my partner? If only I turned back sooner, he might still be alive. I had to find him.

As I walked upon the wide gravel road the lumber company built through the forest, I thought about last night. I recognized the pointlessness of searching in the dark. I also realized that calling my father would only worry him since there was nothing he could do from 800 miles away. No, I got myself into this and I needed to find my way out. A wave of desperation came over me again; I felt nauseous and chilled. This was far more serious than anything I ever faced, but it could be boiled down into two parts: the problem and the solution.

The simplicity of this structure relaxed me. I have a problem and now I just need a solution. I thought more about my father. When I was young and if the family faced a difficulty, my father never gave the appearance of panic. Whatever the problem, he moved deliberately, with calmness. I wondered which came first, the calmness or the appearance of calmness? I realized my longing for my father to take charge cast me in a lesser role, as a follower, and not a leader. I needed to look strong so I could be strong.

After twenty minutes of walking, I found no sign of a logging camp. Without a pack, I could walk four to five miles an hour so I covered a lot more than the half mile. Why did I have such trouble finding logging camps?

I returned to my pack, ate a quick breakfast of Logan Bread and peanut butter and then filled my pockets again with my emergency equipment and the rest of my share of the Logan Bread. I figured the Old Lumber Camp must be somewhere between Mud Pond and Cooper Falls, but I vowed to walk all the way back to Nahmakanta Lake Lean-to if need be. Finally, a decision. What relief I felt. Resolved, I left for my search.

Free of my pack, I walked quickly, randomly blowing three notes on my whistle. I knew that the worst disaster would be my own death; that would definitely ruin the trip. But what if my partner were dead; would I finish the Trail? What would I tell his mother? What a great way to introduce myself. I passed through the area where the old lumber camp should have been. No sign of anybody. I looked left and right for a blue tent; I blew my whistle. I shouted for Rand.

I balanced myself over the sapling shakily bridging the outlet from Mud Pond. I crossed the mouth of the pond on its series of submerged logs: still no sign.

By replacing action for indecision, I shook the cobwebs in my brain. I knew I would find him, one way or the other. My decision gave me energy. I climbed the next hill — nothing. He must have broken his leg or hit his head against a rock. If injured, I would carry him to the Great Paper Road or fix him up in his tent, then go for help. By Mud Pond I concluded that only an injury could have kept him back but I would rescue him.

On I went. I would go all the way back to the lake; I would find him, regardless of his condition. I willed myself to be calm and then let the calm create my confidence. Yesterday, I was so tired and scared I could barely breathe. Today, I was certain I would find him.

From the beginning, I approached this trip with confidence. I assumed a lot — if only I could assume my partner were still okay. I shouted for him. I was nearing the Old Antler's Camp. How could he not reach the Old Antler's Camp after a day of hiking? I blew my whistle. I shouted his name. No answer. I ran. He must be dead, I thought — or worse.

Then I heard a dog bark.

I stopped running. There he was, that crazy malamute, standing in front of a red pack leaning against one of the dilapidated cabins. My partner, yawning sleepily, stepped out into the sun.

"Are you all right?" I said.

"I thought you said 'the Old Antler's Camp.'"

He was okay. Not a scratch on him. No broken bones. Nothing. I looked at his neck but it did not look broken. My mind, so filled with worry and fear, went blank.

"Get your pack on," I said slapping him on the back, "Let's go."

CHAPTER TWO

Fortîtude

JUNE 7

White Cap Mountain Lean-to

We spent last night at the East Branch Tote-Road Lean-to. When there is an East Branch there is usually a West Branch, especially if there is a "Tote Road" in between, connecting the two bodies of water for carrying or "toting" a canoe.

Rand said he could not figure out how to shake the dog after it set off with him. We gave him to some lumberjacks who stopped by the falls next to where I camped and then we continued our walk. He said he heard only the word "Camp" and since the Old Antler's Camp was the only camp named on the first mile post he came to, he figured we meant that one. That the two hikers who left first were not there did not faze him. I cannot fathom how he stopped walking but I fear that if I bring it up we would quarrel and I do not want to sound like an old nag. Nevertheless, I would like him better if I had found him writhing in a creek with a broken leg.

JUNE 10

Drudgery

Drudgery! I'm in pain. I'm wet. I'm muddy and my back hurts. My feet have blisters. My left ankle is swollen. I lost one of my woolen socks. Aside from that — no complaints.

Two nights ago, we camped outside the Gulf Hagas National Scenic Area. Upon arriving, Rand pitched the tent by the Screw Auger Falls while I made dinner. The Gulf Hagas Brook rushes through Screw Auger Falls, a narrow opening flowing into an S-shaped stone sluice. The water sweeps through these falls with a thunderous force, spewing sideways into a stone encircled pool.

After eating, we hiked the five mile circuit along the top of the Gulf Hagas canyon, a place only a shade less breathtaking than the Grand Canyon out west.

Someday, someone will ask, "So, what did you do for fun after you hiked all day?"

"I hiked."

The side trail wound along the top of the canyon overlooking the Pleasant River. Little spruces and firs clung to the edge of the canyon or jutted from rocky crevices many feet below. The needles from the evergreens provided a cushion on the rocky ledge where I paused many times to sit and stare. It was fun walking on this soft path in my leather moccasins. Although I have put them on every day after reaching the destination, this was the first time I hiked in them. I felt like an Algonquin, walking silently through the forest, stalking the unsuspecting wild river.

The force of the water plunging down, between, and over

the rocks churned it buttermilk white. I watched until dark, then carefully made my way back to the campsite.

The next morning, I walked through a cathedral of towering white pines called "The Hermitage." This was a holy place, for it was the last stand of the majestic white pines that had attracted the first ships to reach these shores. The trees in The Hermitage miraculously escaped the merciless axes and chainsaws of the paper and logging companies. (I will never again use an excessive amount of toilet paper.) The Nature Conservancy protects this sanctuary with its dark green ceiling and golden floor. To get there, I hiked a week through mud, rain, and mosquitoes without once crossing a hard paved road. Few people have seen The Hermitage let alone retraced their steps to make sure this stand of white pines still stands. I may never see it again.

Twice within two days I experienced natural beauty so intense all I could do was look in silence and respect. These places transcend tourism. They survived the way God created them. I love walking through gardens to admire how someone like Jefferson or my father used their creativity and knowledge to fashion a place of beauty. The Hermitage and Gulf Hagas are the antithesis. They remain beautiful because no man has tried to make them better. Nor was there litter, graffiti, nor the charred remains of a fire. Those who walked the hundreds of miles to get there left these sacred places untouched, sharing a fellowship with those of us fortunate to follow.

Despite the Hermitage and Gulf Hagas, not all of Maine has been scenic. There have been long sections of the Trail where the blazes faded to resemble lichen. I lost track of these blazes countless times as the swamp-like trail lost itself in the swamp-like forest, forcing me to retrace my steps to where I last spotted a blaze.

Fallen trees have blocked the trail and when I bushwhacked around them, I lost sight of what was trail and what was forest. One time, to avoid getting wet, I leapt across a small brook only to sink to my waist in mud. The incident reminded me of the Lone Ranger episode when he sank in quicksand up to his chest, then whistled for Silver to toss him a lasso. I was able to reach for a tree root and pull myself to drier land.

The guidebook called these trails, "Roads," as in "The Old Lumber Road," suggesting that they were used to haul lumber. Rand commented, "Roads? Why, back home in Virginia, we wouldn't even call these footpaths." Some of the roads have been just a shade more civilized than hacking through the jungle with machetes.

As if I needed another piece of equipment to carry in my overladen pack. I bought a huge expedition pack with all sorts of toggles and patches for running cords through to tie things. Although it came with a large metal external frame, I added a frame extender so I could tie even more things to it.

In the Jeffersonian tradition, I designed a clothes-drying system using a twisted loop of rope through two of the patches on my pack. Here is how this ingenious system was supposed to work. I left with three pairs of woolen socks. I figured I would wear one pair while the second pair would rest snug and dry inside my pack. As for the third, after washing it in a stream with a drop of Dr. Bronner's Hemp Peppermint Castile Soap, I would dry it on my pack while I hiked the next day. The tension caused by forcing two socks into the coils of the ropes would hold them in place.

Brilliant. Everything worked perfectly except for two slight hiccups. The first was that it had not stopped raining, so a day spent drying my socks left them wetter than before. The second flaw with my otherwise fail-proof system was that each step sent vibrations through the pack loosening the coils, so whatever I placed into the drier fell silently onto the Trail. At various breaks, when I removed my pack, I discovered one or even no socks left. Or maybe it was a t-shirt that now lay miles back along the Appalachian Trail. If this keeps up, I will be hiking nude by Massachusetts.

After leaving The Hermitage, the trail took me up and over Chairback Mountain, which required hand over hand climbing up rock ledges with a drop of a thousand feet. At the moment I pulled myself up to the highest ledge, the hinge holding the belt to my pack frame broke. The snapping of the belt jerked my hand off the ledge, almost causing me to fall off the side of the mountain. It didn't, as I was still standing on the lower ledge, but that is

not the point. If I had fallen, I would have stopped writing at this point. (I heard it is not the fall that kills you; it is the sudden impact with the ground that does the damage.)

The hip belt transfers the weight of the pack from the shoulders to the hips and legs. Without it, I would be able to hike no more than five miles a day with a pack as heavy as mine. Although I could still buckle the padded belt around my waist, it is the hinge that transfers the weight. Luckily, through either foresight or laziness, I never shortened my webbed pants belt. By cutting a piece, then sewing it to the worn hinge, I was able to reattach the belt to my pack. I carry a sewing kit, extra toggles and rings, ace bandages, and many other clever, forethoughtful items to use in case my pack breaks due to the excessive weight, made so because of all the clever items I carry.

I sewed the webbing while eating lunch in the lean-to, which I reached a minute after my belt broke. The Chairback Gap Lean-to faces north looking back over the morning's hike. The view looking north is not pleasant — it is desolate. I could see the tops of evergreen trees, granite outcroppings, and distant peaks with no evidence that man had ever passed this way. There were no farms, no villages, no white church steeples that characterize what I think of as New England. Norman Rockwell did not paint this scene; J. R. R. Tolkien did. With the ominous clouds wafting by, sometimes below, sometimes blocking my view, I felt very much alone looking back the way I had travelled.

Tacked to one of the walls of the lean-to was a flier from the Kamikaze Pizza Shop promising "We Deliver — Anywhere!" I wondered how they could deliver all the way up there. I suppose that if you gave them a date, they could drop the pizza off by helicopter. After a lunch of a piece of Logan bread and peanut butter, with a dessert of a papaya stick, I thought helicopter delivery pizza would be worth the bother.

Hiking off the range threatened to be the worst part of an otherwise bleak day. There was no gradual descent. No, that would take planning and care. The blazes followed one after another straight down the side of the mountain. Each step placed tremendous strain on my knees and ankles, jamming my already blistered toes against the front of my boots. After a few steps, I began taking longer and longer strides. Before my toes and ankles could take the full strain of the resistance, I took my next stride and soon found myself leaping down the side of the mountain. The danger of tripping and falling was real but a broken neck could not possibly hurt more than my feet at this point; what is more, the sensation of almost flying was exhilarating. My feet were barely touching the ground as I leapt forward down the mountain, like skiing without snow while carrying a heavy pack. The south side of the mountain was not the steep, rocky, hand-over-hand climb like the north but rather a long slope of trees growing from soft black dirt. I was flying so quickly that before long I reached level ground and slowed my pace to a walk.

I turned to gaze up the steep incline I just flew down. Before I left for the Trail, my doctor gave me two prescriptions. One was Lomitol in case I got dysentery. The other was morphine, in case I broke my leg — maybe by leaping down the side of a mountain. Fortunately, for me, I was able to keep that bottle stashed in my pack.

I caught up with my partner at the Old Stage Road Lean-to

just five miles north of Monson. He was sitting with the silent hiker from Michigan, who was eating his usual dinner of Minute Rice cooked with a bouillon cube. He was in much the same condition as ourselves, tired and sore, so we sat together commiserating. He said that he bruised his ankles descending the steep slope from Chairback.

He could not find the Old Logging Camp, so kept hiking until he reached the Cooper Brook Lean-to, four miles past where I pitched my poncho. When he awoke, he decided that after reaching Monson, he would hitch to Caratunk to pick up his next set of supplies, having miscalculated how long it would take him to cover this stage of the journey. Then, he would hitch back to Katahdin, which he missed climbing eight days earlier because of the rain. At least that was his plan when he set out this morning. After climbing Chairback, that plan changed. The combination of rain, hunger, loneliness, and now his ankles, have finished him off. Tomorrow he will leave Monson for Washington, DC, before returning home to Michigan.

Anyone who hikes the Trail struggles against the environment and themselves. Those who hike to "get away from it all" do not get very far. To survive, we have to move, move when our legs are too tired, when our ankles ache. Those who hike the Trail learn that beauty and serenity are fine sentiments for postcards back home, but they fade as sentiments are wont to do. You can contemplate a sunset without having to climb thousands of feet each day through rain, mud, and mosquitoes. Being a Thruhiker is about moving, not sightseeing, not Zen. If you seek tranquility, try yoga.

JUNE 11

My Kind of Town

Drinking a beer was not the first thing I did upon reaching Monson. When I arrived at the first town along the Trail, I put my clothes in the washer at the town's laundry, walked next door to the post office to pick up our second box of food, and only then did I cross the street to Page's general store for that cold bottle of beer. The simple perks of civilization can turn even a dreary place like Monson into a place of beauty. Beer, fried chicken, and waitresses — things a civilized person takes for granted — these are what kept my legs moving through the swamp they call Maine.

I liken Maine to Paris Island, the Marine boot camp: both teach you how low you can go yet still survive. When you can go days without bathing because as soon as you do you will sink in mud; when you can study a map with both legs covered with mosquitoes, because no matter how many you kill there always will be more; when you no longer hop from rock to rock while crossing a stream because you are already too wet to care; then you have become accustomed to Maine. After Maine, the going gets easy. It has to. Please?

We were not the first Southbounders to reach Monson. According to the trail register at the last lean-to, there were six people ahead of us. I hoped to catch them, not because I wanted to be the first to reach Springer Mountain, but because I never envisioned this hike as a solo expedition. I imagined I would end each day's hike around a campfire with my fellow Thruhikers. Instead I hike alone each day, eat dinner in silence, and fall asleep before dark. Oh well, things will get better as soon as I leave Maine.

We will spend the night in a wooden former church building called "Ken's Hostel." We did not meet Ken as he left yesterday for a wedding and will not return for a week. Watching over the church are two of the Southbounders, Tom and Steve, whose names I read in the trail registers at each lean-to. Tom told us a hiker froze to death in the Chairback Lean-to a few weeks back. (I guess he was waiting for his pizza.) These two were nursing bruised ankles from descending Chairback, the same range that left me with my near death experience. Steve saw a doctor in Greenville who told him only rest could relieve the pain. He seemed resigned that his Thruhiking days were over. I gave him my sympathy but then maintained my distance. Misery loves a companion. I am not going to let myself dwell on negativity; there are all kinds of obstacles to overcome before I finish.

Standing atop Springer Mountain in Georgia was not the foremost goal this past week. My intermediate goal was to fill up on fried chicken and beer. This craving began when we reached the West Pond Branch camp five days ago to retrieve our first box of food. I asked the caretaker if he would sell us some fried chicken for dinner. He stared at me, then shook his head. "There's no fried chicken here."

When I mailed the box to the camp, I pictured a summer camp with a dining hall, tennis courts, and a baseball diamond. Instead, it was a just a collection of grey, dank buildings surrounded by mud.

"Well then how about a glass of milk?"

He did not actually say the needlessly redundant "Take a hike," but I got the message.

After the beer at Page's, my partner and I ate lunch at the one restaurant in town. "I don't need a menu," I told the waitress. "I'll take fried chicken." She suggested I look at the menu because "We don't serve fried chicken." So I settled for a pan fried steak with mashed potatoes and peas, but that evening, after shopping at Page's General Store, Rand cooked up a mess of the best tasting Southern fried chicken north of the Maine border. All right, so he used our cinnamon Bisquick as breading, but it was still finger-licking good.

JUNE 12

Breakneck Ridge Lean-to

I hated to leave Monson, although realistically, it was not much of a town. The lifestyle in these backwater Maine towns seem to be that of survival: surviving the winters, surviving the summers.

In his writings, Jefferson called the big cities "Dens of iniquity." He romanticized the virtue of small town America and country living. Of course, as a slaveholder and plantation owner, he could romanticize his life wherever he resided. Despite his encouragement, the race against rural America began in his time and has continued to the present. Being able to make a living out here in the deep woods of Maine takes hard work under rough conditions and there is not enough money in circulation out here to make this hard work pay. Even owning land out here is not a path toward riches as there is not enough demand for the land to drive up the prices. Eventually, for anyone with the skills and the desire to make more of themselves, moving to the city or to another state has always promised the best opportunity for a secure future, which is why I am fascinated by what keeps some people here or why those who went away came back.

Although I never thought I would, I came back to Monson. About a quarter mile down the road, I realized I forgot to mail my postcards. I laid my pack against a tree and made one last visit to Page's general store to exchange my postcards for an orange-pineapple ice cream cone (well, that and thirty-five cents). Thus my last memories of Monson were sweet.

After mailing my postcards, I strolled south at a leisurely pace, stopping once to look at a group of grosbeaks holding a mass meeting in a shed. There must have been five hundred birds. This was one of the few times I used my binoculars, which otherwise occupied precious space in my pack and added extra weight. If you want to bird watch, take a stroll in your local woods and watch birds; if you want to hike the Trail, hike the Trail.

To look closely at a bird, I take off my pack, remove the rain cover, pull out the binoculars, remove the lens covers, adjust the left eye for my eyesight, then adjust the center dial for the distance — by that time the bird has migrated south. So even though these birds were close enough to see with my naked eye, I went through all the steps. These birds were locals, so they patiently waited for me to justify why I packed these field glasses. They are not heavy in themselves but when added to the weight of the rest of the pack, they were begging me to toss them into a swamp. Once I adjusted the sights, looked at the birds for about ten seconds, I reversed the process and put the glasses away. Maybe I can trade them for some fried chicken?

Just past the shed, I read a memorial plaque dedicated to a private from Monson who died in the Argonne forest during the First World War, the most stupid of all wars.

The harm of WWI was not just that it led to the Communist takeover of Russia and the rise of the Nazis in Central Europe, but it took from the world the beautiful music never made and the scientific discoveries never produced from the young men and women buried beneath its battlefields. I am not going so far as to say that *"War is not the answer."* Sometimes you have no choice. War defeated the Nazis and might prevent the next ideology that thirsts for blood. Grant us the wisdom to know.

If I were king of the world — besides peace among the races and religions and all that kind of stuff — I would make some adjustments to my gear; at least I could control that. These shoes are way too heavy and when they get wet they stay wet. Why not make shoes that have strong soles but light uppers with some extra padding to support the ankle? I do not need to encase my feet in thick leather. Also, all I need is a small pair of binoculars in my pocket, not these huge things built for tracking incoming fighters.

The best piece of equipment I carry is the Sierra Cup. It is wide across the top, made of aluminum, a substance that does not transfer heat, clips to a waist band, and holds ten ounces of chilling spring water or hot soup. With the abundant springs in Maine, I hardly ever use my canteen; all I do is get down to one knee, take a scoop of cold, clear water, then back to walking.

After a nine mile walk, which did my feet little harm, I neared Breakneck Ridge Lean-to. After some of the sheer cliffs I have climbed, I regarded Breakneck with some trepidation, but here was a misnomer if ever there was one. There was no ridge. I just rounded a bend and there it was. The only way I could have broken my neck was from slipping in the mud. Of course, considering I am walking in Maine, that is always a possibility.

Greeting me at the lean-to were two strangers: my partner and Mike, formerly of the trail register team of Mike and Robin. Robin hurt her leg descending Chairback and split to California. Not only do these trail registers provide comments and suggestions — for example, where to shop in the next town — they give us a feel for the people ahead of us. Mike left Baxter Park two weeks before us without climbing Katahdin, due to the weather. The more people I meet, the luckier I realize we were to have climbed the Northern Terminus of the Appalachian Trail.

Out of the Southbounders that I could count, five were injured or quit the Trail and one just completed an extended vacation in the vicinity of Monson. All this happened crossing a range whose highest peak is 2600 feet, half that of Katahdin. A statistician may conclude that the lower the mountain, the more likely it is that someone would get hurt, but Grasshopper, there is a reason for this. Most paths leading up or down mountains, at least in the other forty-nine states, have something called a "switchback," which is when the trail winds up the mountain gradually, sweeping from right to left and back. In Maine, the Trail goes up one side of the mountain and then back down the other — none of this back-and-forth crap for these "Maniacs" (if that is what they call people from Maine.) That is the general rule; the real high mountains like Kathadin have a few switchbacks. The low ones, like Chairback, have none. The Southbounders hurt their ankles on the lower mountains, bracing themselves during the descent. The trail planners in this state comprehend that the shortest distance between two points is a straight line. (Although I cannot argue with the sentiment of getting the hell out of Maine as fast as possible.)

Mike, who spent the last ten days "enjoying the good people of Monson," is back on his journey. He is a funny guy with a lot of stories and an entirely laid back attitude. It will be fun hiking south with him; he probably would not mind hiking together to share thoughts and compare observations. That was, after all, my vision of how to hike the Trail. Maybe I would tire of sharing thoughts and observations. I do not know; I have yet to give it a try.

JUNE 14

Pierce Pond Lean-to

When I awoke the next morning, Mike poked his head out of his sleeping bag, said, "Ciao," and went back to sleep, proving that boot camp is not for everyone.

So I spent another day walking alone. This lean-to sits above Pierce Pond, where I just emerged from chilling my toes. My feet have improved — they now hurt only when I walk. They better heal fast because on Thursday we climb the Bigelow Mountain range with the emphasis on "Big."

Yesterday, while walking along a grassy stretch of the Trail, I came upon nine snakes, each enjoying the sun. They had taken positions about twenty feet apart. I would take a few steps, then, whoosh, a snake sped off the trail; a few more steps, then whoosh went another snake. Some of the snakes were brown with a light underside, while others I recognized as Garter snakes. Also enjoying the sun while munching marsh grass in a nearby pond, a large bull moose stared at me for a while but soon returned to his munching.

As I write, we are about to partake in some munching of our own. Tonight, we will finish our dinner with S'mores for dessert. I bought the fixings in Caratunk, a one-store town on the other side of the Kennebec River. As I walked the last four miles into the village of Caratunk, I wondered what type of people would live in such a small town, so far from civilization. The houses are attractive and well maintained, but how could any worldly person live in a town so far away from the big city lights?

I had dreamt about Mitchell's Country Store in Caratunk for days. The word in the Trail registers was that this was the place to stock up for the tough hiking ahead as well as make the all-important phone call. I pictured a red Coca-Cola cooler, a penny candy counter, and a post office window in the back. I envisioned a tall, thin storekeeper, like the one in *Petty Coat Junction*. Neither Mr. Mitchell nor his store let me down. I spent over an hour there — along with $17. I bought a half gallon of milk, a bag of marshmallows, some chocolate bars, and graham crackers — I was all set. I used the pay phone in the back to call Harold Smith, whom I read about in the *Appalachian Trail News*, to row us across the Kennebec River.

The Trail ends just down the road from Mitchell's store then picks up again on the other side of this very wide river with neither a bridge nor a ford. This is where the hike ends unless you have done a little research. Some hikers have crossed the Kennebec on rafts made from wood and air mattresses. Trying to swim across carrying a pack is not recommended. The Kennebec River is deep and wide with a swift current. I was grateful Mr. Smith came within the hour.

I expected some ornery backwoods potato farmer, but what I found was an educated man, who had seen places, done things, and when the time came to pick a spot of his own in the world, that spot was the one-store town of Caratunk, Maine, where the traffic jams were caused by a slow moving moose and the fish market began at the end of a fishing line.

The old man with skin that looked as tough as moose hide rowed us across the river with short powerful strokes. He told us a bit about himself but like most Maniacs, he was on the taciturn side. About half way across this broad river, he stopped and told us the fee would be five dollars apiece. We were in no position to argue. Caratunk may not offer its inhabitants glitzy nightclubs, but it does have a thriving ferry business.

JUNE 15

Jerome Lean-to

The Lord in all his wisdom made the fly and then forgot to tell us why. — Ogden Nash

Today begins the third week. Amidst the pains in my feet, the sloshing through the mud, the bombardment of the black flies, and the sneak attacks by the mosquitoes, I thought of how much I really enjoy hiking. There is the solitude; the coming upon a creature in the wild; the incredible view of a wilderness lake against a cloudless blue sky (although who knows from cloudless blue skies here in Maine?).

I slept miserably last night. My mistake came after dinner while reading *Ivanhoe*. (Walter Scott modeled the main female character after the daughter of a leader who lived in Philadelphia.) I had taken off my boots and washed my socks for the first time in days. I have suspended all further drying on my pack now that I am down to one and a half pairs — three socks. When I sat cross legged wearing my moccasins but no socks, I noticed about eight black flies affixed to my left ankle bone. I slapped at them and they took off.

The Black fly may be small but its bite leaves a welt that does not itch or burn — or anything — at first. But later, while you sleep, the bite of the black fly itches, bothers, and bewilders until it pops you awake from even the deepest slumber into a frenzy of scratching and rubbing which, although does nothing towards relieving the itch, does help while away the hours.

Nothing I could do would stop the burning that began at my left ankle then shot up my leg. I put my foot in the pond which helped temporarily, but the fire raged again when I got back into my sleeping bag.

After that sleepless night, I walked sixteen miles. Physically, my body aches from the beating it takes hiking all day, every day, while mentally the days have run together: each day, another hike — alone.

I still cannot get over the idea that I am hiking with someone who has done everything he can to hike apart. On that first morning before climbing Katahdin, we left the campsite together to begin our quest. Since then, I have started each day's hike first, but he has caught and passed me without so much as a hello or goodbye. Moreover, I may never — ever — get the Old Antlers Camp out of mind. I mean, if I knew I would be hiking the Trail alone, I would have set about it alone — then there would have been no worry about meeting up at night at some nonexistent logging camp. But I did not set out alone; I left with a partner. I thought that we would hike together, at least within sight and sound of each other.

If this were to have been a solitary hike, why am I here? I never once thought about hiking the Appalachian Trail. This was his idea. I was willing to ride shotgun but I am not even in the same car. This is like getting married and then finding out my spouse does not want kids. Things do not "just work themselves out."

And yet, that is how I set off on this hike.

He must have thought about how this would work but neither of us discussed it. We locked our ideas away, as if afraid to reveal them in case they would shatter under the weight of scrutiny. We lowered our heads and plunged forward rather than take the time to imagine how this walk would play out. Planning the food drops was easy. Figuring out why we were together proved more challenging than climbing Katahdin.

Of all the challenges I face, the one I hate the most is to retrace my steps to find something I lost. This morning, I planned to eat my lunch at the East Cary Pond Lean-to while looking across a succession of lakes toward the twin peaks of Bigelow Mountain. After that, I would hike another ten miles to reach our night's resting place. Just shy of the East Cary Pond Lean-to, after an entire morning of hiking, I discovered I lost my canteen.

I spent a lot of my time preparing for this hike, a lot of

mental time, thinking and imagining. I designed all sorts of contraptions for my pack. Before I left for the Trail, I invented an ingenious water delivery system, the likes of which Jefferson himself would have been proud. Here is how it works or, rather, worked. I tied my green army canteen to my pack in such a way, that, by pulling a cord in one direction, I could lower it enough to drink without taking my pack off. Then, when I pulled the loop the other way, the canteen would return to its place and I would secure the rope to the side of my pack frame using a "Slip Knot." This amazing system suffered only one drawback: the canteen fell off.

I was walking at a good pace, swinging my arms in time with my steps, hearing the cadence of the rustle of nylon, the squeak of the pack, accompanied by the metronome-like cord that swayed in and out of my vision. Step-step; stride-stride. Here goes Sir Alec Guinness marching with the troops to the tune of *The River Kwai*. The metronome made sure I maintained my pace. On I walked, until it dawned on me that I did not pack a metronome: what I saw was the nylon cord that had, until recently, held my canteen.

When I realized what happened, I threw down my pack and retraced my steps. Ten minutes of searching, no canteen. Twenty minutes of searching, no canteen. How many more miles would I add to my already long day? I went back a little farther and then over another hill beyond. Thirty-five minutes of searching: no canteen. Suppose it dropped twenty feet from where I camped last night? Should I retrace the entire day's hike? Suppose it fell twenty feet from where I stopped searching? Could I afford to be so cavalier about one of the most important tools in my possession?

When did I use it last? I filled it that morning but hiking

in June provides ample opportunities to reach into a brook with my Sierra cup for a drink of icy, fresh water, so it was hours since I last needed to take a swig from my canteen. All I noticed was a piece of nylon string, dangling from my pack, and even that clue took a long time to break through my haze.

I walked along oblivious to the world around me. When the blazes disappeared, I kept strolling until I awoke to the realization that I misplaced the Trail again. Yet, it was precisely these dazes that helped me pass the time from day to day and from week to week.

I enjoy the Trail, not for the daily effort of walking — which is more like a job — and not even for the countless vistas and settings I hope to one day revisit. No, this is my chance to contemplate my life.

I remember that short compact oarsmen taking us across the Kennebec River. My life is much like a row boat. I sit in the middle of an expanse of water, oars in hand. I am free to row in any direction, but I sit there, just bobbing in the water. I fear if I row, my life would become one filled with activity but no direction. Will I spend my days looking forward to Friday, my weeks looking forward to summer, my years looking forward to retirement?

Up through high school, I knew exactly what I wanted to do, but the Philadelphia Phillies never got the word. So off to college I went in search of Plan B. I am a man without a plan, willing to charge up any mountain, even if it leads in the wrong direction — hey, at least I am moving. A man without a plan winds up in the middle of a five month walk in the wilderness — without a canteen.

JUNE 16

Avery Memorial Lean-to

I enjoyed my first good night sleep in a while, due to my exhaustion overcoming the itch of the black flies.

A few days back, while I was about to ford the Pleasant River, I stopped to talk with an old timer. I commented, "Looks like we might finally get some clear weather for a change." He said "Most definitely. There was a half-moon last night" — straight out of the Farmer's Almanac. Why did I not know about the half-moon? Come to think of it, I have not seen a moon for weeks as I have collapsed into my sleeping bag in the dreary grey of dusk.

Despite my lengthy sleep last night, we did not get underway until nine; we are both moving slowly. Today we climbed Bigelow and Avery Peaks. I reached the top of Avery at 5 o'clock, spent twenty minutes eating my orange and orienteering, and then hiked into the col, the gap that lies between Avery and West Peak.

This is the first mountain range that we have climbed without immediately descending. Climbing as we do, from the bottom to the peak and immediately down the other side, has given me a different perspective about mountains. I thought the top of a mountain is the peak — it is not. A mountain consists of several parts. First, there is the base: gradually rising and leveling to the foot of the mountain. Next the mountain: rising from the floor to the ceiling, that is, from the base to the summit. Jutting above the summit can be one or more peaks, which is why we needed to reach Baxter Peak, not just Mount Katahdin.

Bigelow is not as high as Katahdin nor as difficult, although climbing with our packs made it every bit as exhausting. Bigelow sits above Flagstaff Lake, two peaks against the sky. From the East Cary Pond Lean-to, where I stopped for lunch two days ago after my unsuccessful search for my canteen, Bigelow looked conical, like a two-headed Mount Fuji. (Not that I have ever climbed Mount Fuji, but I have lived under its shadow for most of my life. My father, who did climb Fuji during the Korean War, hung three posters of different views of the great mountain above my bed, so it became my role model for mountains.)

While I was sitting on the peak looking over the horizon, I felt filled with happiness — joyful. I cannot imagine anything more beautiful than that view. I was sitting at the very top of a mountain with an unbroken view of green forests, glistening lakes, and blue skies.

Maybe because my image of the ultimate mountain was Fuji, I always saw the goal of climbing a mountain as reaching the top to say: "I climbed Mt. Fuji." Certainly when I was climbing Katahdin, all that mattered to me was reaching Baxter Peak, the start of the Appalachian Trail. I have always been flawed in that way. I have always been so goal oriented that the distance to the peak saps the joy that comes from the act of climbing the mountain. The struggles of the past few weeks have made me see that achievement should come from reaching each stage of the mountain, not just the peak. It is not all about what is left ahead, the point of life is to travel beyond where we start and the key to happiness is to find joy along that journey.

I thought of my life after the Trail. I can get by on little. How many leather belts do I need; I have only one waist. The key is not to waste money on frivolous things. If I can keep

THE LONG GREEN TUNNEL

from spending money on junk, I can afford to buy a few items of quality — like a high quality leather belt that will last. As my income grows — and I can control my spending — I can put aside funds so I have a buffer for when I am between jobs. That way, I can afford to look for something better without feeling trapped or I can accumulate the capital necessary to invest in an idea of my own.

Even if I were born with wealth, I would still wish to work for the satisfaction of knowing that I made a difference in the world. I want to accomplish something; something of value. An English teacher, Irv Rotman, at Central High School in Philadelphia (not Little Rock) told us that a famous comic actor (loved by the French, oddly enough) said "I don't care what my son does for a living as long as he is the best." My teacher then asked, "What? The best murderer? The best robber?"

We got his point.

I often hear we should do what we love. So, I have made a list of the things I love doing: playing baseball, having sex, playing with dogs, kissing, making out, eating, sitting in front of a fire, reading, solving math puzzles — pretty much in that order. I love doing most things that I get lost doing, where the time slips away unnoticed. I do not have the talent to get paid to play baseball. I have not figured out how to get paid for having sex; probably lack the talent there too. Reading and math puzzles? I will need to figure out how I can get paid to do that.

We all are equal in the eyes of the Lord, but some jobs are more important than others. Not all of us can become the President of the US, but a complicated world such as ours relies on people spending their days providing value to others. Where would we be without people to take away our trash without scattering it over the street? How can we live in a city without people to keep our busses and trains running? What job, if performed well, and if ethical, is not important to the complex clockwork of our modern society?

If I were the president of a company I would make sure to eat lunch with the employees, not just the top executives. Every job matters. Each person deserves respect for what they contribute. When they do their part, we get to do our part better. If the fast food worker does not deliver a meal on time, then the person we need to deliver a letter across town may have waited too long at lunch to get the job done. That fast food worker may not have done her job well because despite working two jobs, she cannot earn enough money to raise her children with dignity. Not only does she deserve our respect, we, as a society, need her to focus on raising healthy, well-adjusted kids and not living her life on the edge of disaster. The first step for all of us is to show respect to everyone who works hard and provides value. But let us not make that the last step, either.

For me to enjoy my life, I want people to show up at my funeral and miss me. (At least those who will have lived long enough to attend, as I hope to outlive most of my contemporaries.) Beside the satisfaction of having made an impact on the world, there is also the satisfaction that comes from waking each morning excited for the day ahead. Maybe the secret is not to do what we love but to learn to love what we do. I want a career that fills me with joy, the same feeling of awe and gratitude I felt on Avery Peak. (Although too much joy will mean that my life will go by too quickly since miserable times seem to last longer.)

As I sat on the peak, the sun broke through a cloud at such an angle and with such suddenness that the vista was littered with what looked like broken pieces of glass, the sun's reflection on the innumerable ponds and lakes below. Someday, I will return to one of those cold, clear lakes to coax a trout onto my fishing line. Perhaps, one day, I will spend a week in a cabin as I promised myself each day, as I hiked past one place of unspoiled beauty after another. Even though my choice in life may never coincide with Mr. Harold Smith's, hiking the Trail has given me a taste of his life. Far from the flashing lights of the big city, a person learns to find joy in other things such as the sun glistening off lakes. I search and I continue to search. And if the miles — and the Harold Smiths — change me for the better, I guess it was worth a canteen here or there.

JUNE 18

Crocker Cirque Campsite

The clouds hung low over the village of Stratton, but for once the rain stayed away. I could see from my motel room this day would be overcast at best. It poured yesterday, forcing us off the Bigelow Mountain Range. It took two hours to hitch into Stratton, so that was miserable, but our spirits needed the chance to sit out the storm. Stratton was a one-diner town where we prepared ourselves for the big challenges yet to come.

But that was yesterday. Today, after only one and a half hours of hitching, we got a ride back to the Trail. The sky was still overcast, but the rain stayed away.

About halfway up Crocker Mountain, I walked into clouds. Mystical: the sensation of walking through a phantom forest where the trees behind vanished with each step to be replaced by still more ahead. Upward and upward, I walked into denser and denser fog. At times, I stopped, losing sight of my feet. Mosquitoes don't like the fog; they left me alone. It was cool in the clouds, comfortable. There was no view, only white mist, thinning in some places, growing thicker in others. The fog would clear for an instant and I would see a gray Canada jay to my left. We stared at each other at eye level. The pine tree he perched upon began far below the unseen cliff. At this altitude only conifers grow. Despite the fog, the white blazes of the trail stood out against the dark bark of the pine and spruce trees. I was grateful for this. Losing my way up here might mean falling to where the pine trees grow.

I was carrying my heaviest load yet, having stocked up for nine days in Stratton including two Italians, or what they call a hoagie in Philadelphia. Rand and I ate lunch together after leaving Stratton, something we seldom did, but since we got back to the Trail at noon, we were not far apart by lunchtime.

We hiked only seven miles after Stratton, but that included a 3400 foot net gain in elevation — an incredible climb over seven miles. Net gain is a bit misleading. It does not take into account all the rises and falls that go with hiking, only the change from the bottom to the top of the climb. Within the first ten minutes, I changed out of my long pants and put away my down parka and windbreaker. I was burning up. I was like a locomotive chugging over the mountains full throttle, burning coal, whistling steam — I burned that sandwich within five minutes. (From the burps — believe me — I knew it was the sandwich.) Despite the steepness, the day went smoothly. I felt tired at the end but not sore.

Down here, writing before dinner in the hollow called Crocker Cirque, I see the changes in my body. When I started the trail my thighs were big, but not well defined. At first, my thighs shrunk, as each day's exertion burned off more of the fat. But soon, the swelling muscles made my thighs even bigger than before. While pitching our tent amidst the birch trees and the fog wetted grass, I could see the muscles rippling through my legs, stretching the bottoms of my shorts.

Traveling south from Katahdin gradually molds the hiker. First comes Katahdin — a very tough climb but done without packs. Then comes Whitecap — not tough, but with packs. Then comes Chairback — the guidebook calls it "the toughest climb between Katahdin and the Mahoosics." Then the Bigelows, and so on.

I thought I would train for the Trail by carrying metal weights in my backpack on walks through the woods near my house. But, the best way to train to hike long distances, over high mountains, carrying heavy packs is to hike increasingly longer distances, over increasingly higher mountains, carrying increasingly heavier packs. Not to mention the weights ripped a hole in my brand new blue backpack, which I repaired using grey duct tape.

More than my legs have been growing. Losing my way, sinking to my waist in mud, searching for my partner — all have required me to make decisions. At first, I wished there were someone to lean on, someone who would assume the responsibility. I wanted my father to make decisions for me, but I am the one who committed to this hike. Although I might call out for help, no one else can give me the answers, so I am forced to learn to stay calm and decide. I am the one hiking through the Maine Woods. If I want to lie in my sleeping bag all day and say "Ciao," I can do it. Nobody controls my life here but me. Of course, I am the one who would starve when the food runs out, but that is independence too. The ultimate freedom, the freedom to move or to starve. Freedom does not guarantee happiness, but not having freedom sure brings unhappiness. That is why some men drink to excess or blow themselves up on busses. They are not free or they have not made the connection that freedom requires responsibility. Those who live lives of quiet desperation wind up committing stupid, hideous acts. Whatever the cause one proclaims for self-destruction is never the reason. Facing the freedom to lie in my sleeping bag and starve offers tremendous power, the power to control my own life. Recognizing that I must suffer the consequences of my own action is liberating, although frightening.

When I matriculated at the University of Virginia, I was admitted into the Echols Scholar program. This honor meant I could take any course I wanted without requirements or prerequisites. I selected a first semester curriculum of mostly upper level courses. The dean said, "You will have a lot of reading to do but I am sure you will find the semester most interesting." That semester turned out be an example of too much freedom. Not only did I earn poor grades, I did not learn much because I was overwhelmed. I was given so much freedom I drowned.

Although challenges may grow us, when we are young and stupid, or in kinder terms, inexperienced and naïve, we need engaged advisors to question our choices so we understand why we chose the way we did. Some challenges help us grow and some rip us apart. The trick is to grow from accepting ever increasing challenges.

One does not have to hike the Appalachian Trail to face unpleasant outcomes. The student who lulls in bed will flunk. The mechanic who lulls in bed will get fired. In the end, we will all starve. But lulling in a sleeping bag, watching the rain drip off the lean-to, has two differences: solitude and a nearer end. No other voice pierces the early morning to warn me of the consequences; no alarm clock wakes me, no wives, parents, children, nor employers remind me of my responsibilities. I have no responsibility to anyone and no one waits for me at the next town.

I am keenly aware that a few hours delay each day, will cause me to run out of food, not when I am eighty, but by next week. I see my consequences clearer than most others can. That is independence.

Wealthy Colonial American youths, like Thomas Jefferson,

sailed to Europe to further their education. But the real learning from The Grand Tour came from the independence of being alone in a foreign land. My vision of The Grand Tour did not include mud and mosquitoes. I wanted to spend my junior year travelling through Europe, but the chance of winning a scholarship disappeared as I ran out of time. I was disappointed but my friend saw an opportunity. He said to me, "I am glad you missed going to Europe. There is something I have always wanted to do and there is no one I would rather do it with than you."

Thus, I accepted Rand's invitation to help him live his dream. Once my dream fell through, why not bum a ride on someone else's dream? At least it was a dream. So I thought. Now, here I am.

The Trail does not have the cafés of Paris, the art galleries of Florence, the sun drenched beauties lying on the sun drenched beaches of Saint-Tropez, but it does offer its own set of challenges. So I missed learning about art and architecture, but I have encountered and survived some difficult situations. Each challenge has prepared me to handle the next problem: more than my thighs have grown.

I wanted to step out of the ordinary to see my life. The Trail is both challenging and out of the ordinary. Perhaps I should have thought more before signing on or at least given my dream some more effort, but here I am, so I better make the most of it.

What am I here for? I hike for beauty. I hike for tranquility. I hike to accept and meet challenges. I also hike for the independence of finding my own way through the fog. Each day I make the choice. Each day I leave my sleeping bag for another day in the clouds.

JUNE 19

Apocalypse Trail

There are people who want to make a religious experience out of hiking. There are those looking for the Burning Bush on Mount Katahdin and I am sure some have tried walking across the Kennebec River — without a bridge. But personally, I have not awaited the Apocalypse on the Trail, even though I now admit that the Trail's seclusion, serenity, and high-altitude bring a person closer to God — and to his help.

I started the day wet. Not long after starting I fell into a swift, though shallow, river. Before I crossed, I worked out one of two possible solutions for leaping across the river from rock to rock, but it required leaping at full stride with no pauses for deliberation. I took several steps back and then ran at full speed to the bank leaping for the first rounded stone jutting from the water. I hit off that with my left foot and then caromed to the right, momentarily touching down on a rock, then left, then right when I jumped to a large rock, safe I thought, but it teetered under my weight. Fortunately, I was able to jump to another rock unscathed. Unfortunately, that rock also proved unstable, flipping over and sending me headfirst into the Carabassett River.

The day went downhill after that — although the direction of hiking proved otherwise — and by 6 o'clock I was still a long mile away from a night's rest. Having hiked for hours already, I could not muster the energy to climb Poplar Ridge.

I have battled hunger for at least a week. We eat three meals a day but they are of the same size as those we ate at the beginning of our journey. I was satiated during the first week but now I perpetually crave nourishment and get weaker. My legs have grown but the rest of me has wasted away. I can barely lift my pack; instead I have to swing it upon my knee, then quickly slip my arm through the shoulder strap and hitch it up so I can get the other arm into its strap before it falls.

Each day, I have looked up trails that require thousands of feet of climbs. The Trail guide calls the next thirty-mile section, the Mahoosucs, the "roughest hiking in all of Eastern United States," and I have already hiked through mountain ranges that were devastatingly difficult.

Although the pack I carried out of Stratton contained mostly food, I had to make that cache last for nine days. This meant I carried a heavier load over more miles per day without increasing the size of our meals to compensate for this greater expenditure of energy.

I have been operating under the steam engine theory. So long as I keep shoveling fuel into the engine, it will run. But macaroni may not provide the same nourishment as a steak, an apple, or a spear of broccoli. Maybe they represent the same calories, but I can feel the difference on a day we eat real meat and vegetables versus a day fueled by some form of pasta, rice, or potato. I suspect that not all calories are equal. What I need right now is a hoagie. A hoagie combines all sorts of meats and cheese on a crusty roll — and it has vegetables too — like lettuce, onions, tomatoes, and crushed peppers. It is a perfect food.

Writing about food just made me relive the conversation from last night. I do not want to dwell on it by writing about it, but sometimes I feel we are two strangers who happen to travel along the same path. In fact, meeting up with a stranger would be a lot better since we would hold no expectations.

After slipping into the Carabassett River this morning, I spent the rest of the day climbing up one side of a mountain and then down the other. My legs ached with fatigue and I began to walk in a daze, listlessly putting one foot in front of the other. I tried to think of *The Little Engine that Could* and chanted, "I think I can, I think I can," but even that could not keep me going. After a day of wet drudgery, I stood at the bottom of Poplar Ridge, one steep mile away from the Poplar Ridge Lean-to where I might enjoy a much-needed night's rest.

"The ridge is only 2500 feet high," I said, "a mere pup compared to the surrounding mountains."

The concentric circles on the topographical map made the ridge look like a black smudge. Poplar Ridge loomed over me like a muddy fortress. The Trail planners in Maine wasted no thought on switchbacks to make the ascent more gradual; no, this was yet another assault straight up a mountain on dirt that bore weeks of rain and was ready to give way under foot. Although the rain stopped, the clouds still hovered ominously, threatening a downpour the moment I say, "It could be worse; it could be raining."

I gazed up the steep trail. "Just a little further along the Trail, farther up the hill, 'I think I can,'" but my body said, "No. You can't." At some point "fatigue makes cowards of us all" and I had reached that point. Alone, I would have unrolled my sleeping bag on the forest floor and gone to sleep. But my partner was somewhere ahead, probably at the lean-to by now, and I would not stop until I reached him, so I started to climb. Reaching for saplings, I pulled myself upward, digging into the soft soil with whatever I could: my hands, my feet, my knees, even my chin. From the first sapling I reached for a second and from that a third, but the strain of carrying too heavy loads, over too high mountains, on too little food overwhelmed me. My head reeled and I missed my next hold. Lunging forward, I grabbed for the next tree, but stepped on an exposed root, slipped, and went sprawling down the slope with my backpack dragging behind me. Once more I found myself at the bottom of the ridge, but this time with my arms and feet tangled with my pack.

"Dear God, please help me."

Forcing myself to stand, like a punch drunk fighter, I renewed my assault. But before I took my first step, I looked down at my feet. There lay a long stick with a knot six inches from the end. I picked it up, and clutching the knot, put my weight on it, testing the stick's strength. It held. Through the stupor of my fatigue, I dug the stick into the soft earth and, leaning forward, hoisted myself upward. I did not need the sap- lings anymore and I could stand rather than crawl. With the help of my walking stick, I steadily climbed to top of the ridge, where thoroughly exhausted — but triumphant — I let out a yell of relief. A chill passed through my body as the air blew against my wet clothes. The forest filled with a heavy silence; even the trees stood still. No longer did

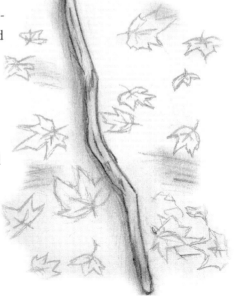

I hear the call of the White Throated Sparrow. Then, for what seemed like the first time, I saw the sun. I watched, silently, as the clouds separated, revealing blue skies above and green forests below.

"Thank you."

I knew I must go on, but still, I waited. Suddenly a woodpecker, tapping for food in a dead tree, broke the long silence. I knew I could go on.

"Thank you."

JUNE 20

Moose Moo

After reaching the lean-to last night, my partner handed me my share of dinner and then walked away in silence. I showed him my new walking stick but he raised his eyebrows as his only response. Help me, someone, anyone, to understand what I am doing here.

It poured again last night, followed by a cold front. Although I walked only eight miles, that distance included three high peaks and a three mile walk above the timberline. I started the day dressed in long pants and a wool shirt. The shirt I could unbutton, but the pants, which I left on, dragged me down. This burden, along with an ample carryover of yesterday's exhaustion, caused me to labor with every step. After two hours, I stopped to eat lunch, read two chapters of *Ivanhoe,* and change into shorts. This felt better, but I could not shake the dead feeling that penetrated my legs, requiring me to take numerous rests.

I crossed the Horn and the Saddleback peaks today. From

the side, the mountain resembles a western saddle. The top of the ridge is treeless. Walking through the dense thicket of shrubs and wiry plants reminded me of the arctic tundra, where an intense active world exists within inches of the ground. It felt like November on top of this arctic world; the word "exposure" crossed my mind which was why I dressed so warmly when I set off.

As I walked, I thought about how nice it will be to see my parents in Vermont. I am hiking for independence, for the expression of my rugged individualism. And yet I have a close family which makes me who I am. So I am both independent and interdependent. My search for independence does not have to destroy the bonds between my parents and me, although my assertion of independence does alter them. I am at the doorstep of my future, the past is my home but now I must go out into the world. My future looms important in the distance, yet the path remains cloaked in clouds.

Everyone has to make choices. We all start with promise, yet only a few will scale the heights of wealth, fame, and success. I just wish I knew the secret that separates one wanderer — who fulfills his dreams — from the next who spends his life searching for that one break. There must be something in the as yet unformed college-aged brain that shapes the personality, establishing its direction. There are times I can assert my personality to take me in a given direction, but there are other times when I feel incapable of acting decisively. I worry that I will waste my life if I lack a firm direction, so here I am, in Maine, trying to figure the path to choose. Am I kidding myself thinking I will be able to solve my life when I am so removed from my real life? Although I wake each day to hike south, I am really searching for the direction my life will take. If I can get there by thinking about it, then I will need all the quiet time these next five months of solitary confinement will avail. Will the Trail mature me faster than five months spent at some alternative course of action? I should have set up a control group.

Of all the super powers I could have, the one I want the most is the ability to rewind. So law school does not work out as expected. Rewind. Now I will apply to medical school. If that does not work out: rewind. I would take that over X-ray vision anytime.

I had a run in today. The first time I saw a moose was by the entrance to Baxter State Park. The driver, who picked us up in Oldtown, dropped us off there after a hundred mile ride. We sat in the back of his pickup truck with two massive Bernese Mountain dogs (just about the most beautiful dogs in the world). We were all set to try hitching the remaining eight miles to the campground,

when the ranger poked her head out of the entrance booth and offered us a ride once she finished her shift. We walked off the road to a picnic table which overlooked a series of ponds leading to the incredible form of Mount Katahdin, rising like Mount Fuji above the Maine plain. There I saw my first moose eating marsh grass. Even from that distance I could tell a moose was a huge animal, one I would never wish to meet face-to-face.

We came butt-to-face with a moose later that night. During the ride to the campground, a moose entered the roadway and slowly meandered north for what seemed like an hour. We followed at a safe distance, driving at the pace of the moose, which in this case was no more than four miles per hour, a good speed for a meandering moose, but not so great for a car, especially as the sun was setting. The driver of the car that drove up behind us was not as interested in the backside of a moose as in getting to the campground. He tried to speed the procession by flashing his lights and tapping his horn. This greatly agitated our driver who would have none of that big city behavior. She moved to the center of the dirt road, preventing the car from passing, until the moose safely headed back into the woods. Then she moved over to let the other car pass, but not before admonishing, "There's a speed limit he-ah and the animals have right of way."

As I walked down from the ridge, I observed the results of centuries of bad lumbering practices. The thicket on either side of the Trail consisted of dense stands of narrow trees, making meandering off the path impossible either for a Thruhiker silhouetted by a large blue pack or for the even larger woodland creature, the moose.

Every step I took along the steep narrow path emitted

a squish or a squash as I stepped along a chute laden with moose moo. As unpleasant as this seemed, it occurred to me that this was the Maine moose's main thoroughfare. The next bull moose trotting down this slope could easily gore me with his huge rack of antlers, trample me beneath his hooves, and leave me oozing amongst the moo. The thicket, as daunting a barrier as any bamboo jungle in Viet Nam, would offer no escape. A moose can reach seven feet just to his shoulders, with a huge head and broad, pointy antlers, while weighing as much as a car. I walked as fast as I could to get out of the moose chute, using my newly acquired walking stick as a ski pole to keep from slipping in the black muck.

From the time I left Kathadin, I followed white rectangular blazes, two inches by six inches, painted six feet high on trees. When I reached one such blaze, I usually could spot the next. Every so often, I spied a double blaze, one six-inch blaze over another, signifying a turn. What the double blazes do not signal is whether I should turn right or left. So, I would select a direction to turn and look for the next blaze. If I did not see one, I would turn around and look the other way.

Sliding and trotting down the hill to avoid an oncoming moose, I saw the double blaze ahead. A few strides later, I stepped onto a jeep road; safe at last. For whatever reason, I turned left. I took one step and then stopped, coming nose-to-nose with a moose. Fortunately, this was not an adult moose; he looked like a teenage moose. His rack was not huge and he was thinner than the other moose I watched from afar. Nevertheless, he was big enough to do some damage if I did not handle the situation carefully; moreover, teenagers are hard to predict. I dared not make any sudden movements

or noise. I slowed my breathing and tried to calm my pulse. We stood nose-to-nose — although his was a much larger nose. My eyes and nose are close together, whereas his nose protruded far below his eyes, which strained to keep me in sight, so close to his snout was I. Although our noses practically touched —his was a really long nose observed from this distance — there was a lot more to his body. Think of a large, scraggly horse — with horns.

What could I do? One head butt from him and I would be flat on my back, ready for trampling.

I looked at him and he looked at me.

Both of us, no doubt, were wondering what type of creature we just encountered. (I mean, I knew it was a moose, but what type of moose: friend or foe?) This moose was much taller than I and his eyes were fixed on me.

I carry a large blue pack that completely frames my head

and body. I wear a red hat on top of my head and I have a three week beard. He, on the other hand, was wearing the fur God gave him.

He looked at me and I looked at him.

I did not know what he would do next and, if he is writing in his journal, he is admitting he had no idea what I was going to do either. I knew I could not get past him and it appeared he could not figure out how to get past me. Allowing my gaze to look down the road, I was no longer sure I needed to get by him; I could see trees but no blazes. I cannot vouch for where he needed to go.

I looked at him and he looked at me.

I needed to remove myself from this situation without startling him as I did not need to provoke a head butt from a thousand pound moose. So I carefully took a step backwards with my right foot. No head butt. I then took another step with my left. No head butt. The moose got with the plan; he took a tentative step backwards, first one hoof, then another. I matched his steps and raised him one. He again stepped backwards. Slowly I turned to my right and he turned to his left. Then I saw the blazes, and headed off in the opposite direction, not daring to look back until I walked some yards down the road. When I looked back I could see his backside as he trotted in the direction from whence he came.

"Good bye, old friend."

I waved, hitched up my pack, and continued my journey south.

CHAPTER THREE

Friendship

JUNE 22

Hungry Hearts

How did we get to this point?

Let me go back to the night before we climbed Mt. Katahdin, my partner made me promise, "No matter what happens between us, we communicate. Without communication, we will not last."

"Yes, we must communicate," I said.

"Promise you'll communicate."

"I promise I'll communicate."

We then gazed at the night sky and talked about shooting stars and Carlos Castaneda who said that all the paths we take are the same so "we must follow the one with heart." I nodded in understanding but I had no idea how to find a path with heart.

The next day we started our hike. Less than a mile into it, the dense trees surrounding both sides of the path opened to reveal a huge swale between ridges in which it looked like the finger of God flicked the forest, knocking over thousands of trees, their grey, dried trunks leaning against each other like rows of dominos. The ranger called it a "blowdown" and the resultant dried trees, stranded in the air for years instead of rotting on the ground, creates a fire hazard.

Blowdowns are not caused by winds, but by poor logging practices. The dense thickets of saplings grow in weakened soil, weakened because the first clear cut exposed the soil to the rains and melting snow which washed away eons of topsoil. Without the shade of mature trees, the saplings crowded together. The denseness of this after-growth prevented trees from falling to the ground. Without the rotting trees, the soil remained barren of organic matter, thus unable to offer the proper soil to allow the roots to support strong, vital trees. So whenever one tree lost its foothold, it fell against others, toppling them until they formed a blowdown stretching hundreds of feet.

I found myself mesmerized not just by the terrible destruction but also by the vastness of the view from the vantage point we reached just minutes into our two thousand mile hike. I stood there, staring, until my partner, my friend, broke the trance when he communicated, "I hope you do not intend to stop every time I do." And with that he walked off.

That is the problem with communication. When one person communicates; the other person has to listen. My first reaction was to say "You talking to me?" But it happened so unexpectedly. When I picked my chin off the ground, all I saw was a green hat and a red pack heading into the woods. I stood there all alone.

For a moment I thought of turning back to the campsite. The path ahead looked bereft of heart for me.

Five hours later, I reached the top of Katahdin and came to a sign marking the Northern Terminus of the trail. Looking north, I could see another peak connected by a narrow land bridge known as the "Knife Edge" promising a sheer drop of a thousand feet on either side. I did not intend to start my hike by falling off a ledge that was not even part of the official Trail; if I am going to fall off a cliff, I wanted it to count. Ironically, thinking about it over two hundred miles later, crossing the Knife Edge would have been an interesting experience. As there are no trees on Kathadin, just lichen-covered rocks, we would have hiked in view of each other, something we have not done since. When my partner said back at school, "There is no one else I would rather hike the Trail with than you," he must have been talking in the abstract sense, not the actual process of hiking.

We walked 238 miles in three weeks to reach the Elephant Mountain Lean-to — basically keeping to ourselves, in our own separate worlds.

Two nights ago, we found ourselves camping near the Piazza Rock Lean-to — camping — because the lean-to was filled with a Boy Scout troop. There are several types of hikers. There are groups who hike small sections over a few days. There are week-long hikers, arriving and leaving the Trail on weekends to fit the experience into their schedules. And then there are the Thruhikers, those attempting to hike the whole thing, starting either in Maine or in Georgia. The Northbounders have left Georgia by now, as they have to finish before the winter hits. Meeting them will not mean I will have someone to hike with, as we will be walking into each other, but if the timing works, we can share a lean-to for a night and at the very least, we can chat about our similar experiences.

As we camped at Piazza Rock, a strange thing happened:

all through an unprecedented evening and night, the rain stayed away — I was afraid my sinuses would dry. But normalcy returned to the Maine woods the next morning as the rain fell in full force under a gray sky. When I began to strike the tent, my partner sent me away.

"Leave the tent alone, I'm not hiking in the rain."

"I may not be a practicing meteorologist, but I do know that as long as you hike in Maine, you'll be hiking in rain."

"I'm sitting this one out," he said.

"Then I will have some food waiting at the next lean-to, but don't wait all day."

What was a little rain, after all? If my partner insisted on sitting out every rain, he would be an old man before setting eyes on New Hampshire. After three weeks, I wanted out of this state. The more time we watch the rain, the longer we have to stay in Maine.

I wore my poncho and rain chaps all day. The poncho limited my lateral vision, while the clouds darkened the sky. With no sun to pierce the forest canopy, the color was gone. The falling rain and the muddy ground soaked me no matter what I tried; I wore the poncho to keep the mosquitos away.

Whenever the rain paused, I found a rock to sit on, pulled out Sachar's book *Modern Jewish History,* and munched some gorp. We all know about the Bible and we know the history of the twentieth century, but I do not know much about the years that connected the two. This book bridges the gap, from the perspective of the Jewish people. It is not a humorous book but it does explain a lot about why the world is what it is today. Not talking to anyone — not hiking with anyone — made me crave books. Sachar is my third book in three weeks of hiking by day and falling asleep when the sun set.

That is, of course, when there was a sun. I planned to dry my socks each day on my ingenious clothes drier. If I hiked during winter, I would have been okay because wool retains heat even when wet. But this was the summer and a wet sock feels like a wet sock. Moreover, the grit from sinking too many times to my knees in mud have formed a deep-seated relationship with these socks. They worked on me like eighty-grit sandpaper, scraping my ankles raw.

Each of my previous days involved steep climbs. I have been so tired of late that my head burns from fatigue, but there are no burnout centers on the AT. Thankfully, the hike to Sabbathday Lean-to was an inbetweener, a connecting piece of land between two mountain ranges with just some rolling hills along the way.

I have developed a better way to hike uphill; I call it "The Method." On steep climbs, I have to lift my knee up and forward, put my foot down, then lift my body using the muscles in the area around the knee — step climbing. After too much of this, the muscles supporting the knee, thigh, and ankle grow fatigued. Climbing is more tiring than walking — nothing newsworthy about that. Consequently, what I have learned to do on inclines is to not lift my knee. Instead, I keep my knee bent, but rigid, and use my butt muscle to move my entire leg up the incline. I am butt walking rather than knee walking. The Method does not apply to steep climbs nor normal ambling, just what I would call climbing a ramp. It saves energy and reduces wear and tear. When I get back, I will patent it.

Every now and then as I walked along in the monotony of rain and mud, I passed the shores of a boreal swamp. Unlike a lake, a swamp does not invite. Its murky waters hold neither treasures of trout nor the promise of a swim. Large clumps of sphagnum moss dot the water along the base of the skeletal remains of trees that perished under the befouling waters. The melancholy picture matched the dreariness of the day. I moved on.

The furry little woodland creature, the beaver, created these swamps after building elaborate dams across streams. Because of their busy deeds, the beavers have changed the appearance of thousands of acres of Maine wilderness. Cheeky devils. The water undermines the remaining trees which fall over and rot in the swamp. Eventually, the beavers give up repairing the dam of their ancestors and it too rots, releasing the water and draining the swamp. Then new trees grow along a wilderness stream until a new beaver comes along with a song in his heart and the dream to build a homestead to raise a family.

I was already feeling dreary without the landscape giving me additional cause. Last week, we restocked our supplies in Stratton; I bought peanut butter, margarine, and honey — our staples. My partner bought a tin of fudge and a bag of cookies. "Good thinking," I said to myself, "If he buys dessert, I'll buy lunch." So, I bought two Italians.

After hitching back to the Trail in yet another Maine monsoon, we set off through the forest. After about fifteen minutes, just as the terrain began to climb, we stopped for lunch. Sitting on some smooth granite rocks, covered with blue lichen and green moss, under a canopy of trees that kept us fairly dry, we ate fresh rolls filled with Italian meats and cheeses that had warmed enough to emit their tastes and aroma. My partner, by his own admission, grew up on foods like boiled ham, Wonder Bread, and Miracle Whip. Meats cured with garlic, Italian rolls and seasonings were new to him.

That night, in Crocker Cirque, we finished one of the meals I packaged months before, something I named "Long Day Stew." It was filling — it consisted of a can of tuna fish and parmesan cheese mixed into a cup of noodles — well, maybe filling for one person. It came with two papaya sticks for desert. I suggested, "Let's save these for tomorrow's hike and eat some of the fudge instead." My partner looked at me as if I were some kind of thief.

"The fudge is private stash — if you wanted some, you should've bought some."

"But I bought lunch."

"And I thanked you for it."

He took his papaya stick and walked away. I tried my best not to let this exchange affect me but with each passing day, my resentment grew. "Communication," he said. But what sort of communication could atone for such pettiness. Boy was I angry. I was hungry, constantly hungry — and I was angry.

I spent the days since either alone or existing in silence with Rand. When I reached the Sabbathday Lean-to, I figured that my faster walking partner would arrive shortly. I read for a while and made a cup of tea. Not having dry clothes to change into, I slipped into my sleeping bag. The tea warmed me, but I remained hungry and now my partner would hold up our meal because of his pettiness. A little rain. I ate a tablespoon of peanut butter to keep me warm.

In the time I waited, I could have hiked the five miles to the next lean-to, and been that much closer to leaving Maine. I sat and I waited. After an hour, I wondered if something happened to him. But no, I chased down that trail before; I would not go back. Just thinking about the incident of the Old Logging Camp made me seethe. I refused then and there to worry about him again, stubbornly holed up as he was in his tent, trying to outlast Maine's never ending rain.

My Dad would be disappointed in us. If you have a gripe about someone, he would tell you to spill it out, deal with it. He would say, "The unspoken words become a bigger problem than the problem." Communicate and the whole world will communicate with you. My Dad would also point out that when you think the problem is about fudge, it usually is about something else. I tend to think about a conflict, stew on it, and think some more. I can bear with a blister or even a shard of wood sticking through my thigh better than I can suffer through the endless chatter in my head that robs me of the enjoyment from, well, in this case, an otherwise dismal, wet, and rainy day.

I threw dinner into the pot and cooked it over a low flame. At ten minutes to seven, he walked up to the lean-to.

"You break a leg, or what?" I communicated.

"Why don't you drop dead?"

After exchanging these pleasantries, our conversation took a turn for the worse. We touched on all those things that accumulated over the past few weeks. Every time he voiced a complaint, I got insulted or became defensive. He took my remarks in the same vein.

I accused him of breaking the spirit of a partnership by hoarding fudge; he said I was an oppressive bully who took without asking. "But I shared my stuff with you," I said.

"You didn't give me the chance to share; you just assumed that what I bought was yours. It is not like you don't have your own private stash."

"What's that supposed to mean?" I asked.

"I want to switch," he said. "You carry the tent and I'll carry the peanut butter."

"What do you need the peanut butter for, Mr. Private Stash? Besides, that peanut butter keeps me alive every time you decide to go on a vacation. I have to carry the stove, the fuel, and the rest of the staples. Combined, their weight exceeds that of the tent."

"That's not always true. Each day we eat the food, and we burn the fuel, so the weight you carry drops. Not only does the tent weigh the same every day, because of the rain, its weight actually increases. I poured a cup of water off the tent today."

"Well then, if you poured a cup of water off, you weren't carrying it — were you? Eight ounces of water? I don't know how you manage to stand under all that weight. "

Communication certainly does wonders for a relationship. By the time we went to bed, we stopped shouting. We also stopped talking or looking at each other. Admittedly, I become just a tad sarcastic when I get angry (in many respects, my wit is at its best at the height of an argument, although that usually doesn't help matters). But my partner uses his anger by not hiking together, by not sharing, and by disregarding me.

What a pair we made.

What did I think this hike would be like? We never discussed the actual hiking aspect. He invited me to hike with him and I agreed. Now that I have time to think about it, just because I missed the deadline for the Rotary scholarship did not meant there were no other opportunities to study abroad. But I cut myself off from pursuing an alternative plan. Instead of his plan, I could have explored other options. Instead, I just gave up my dream at the first impasse.

Did I lack the strength to say, "I am flattered by your offer but give me some time to think about it?" Once I accepted the hike, I poured my energy into hiking: I read books, magazines, newsletters, and spoke with experts at backpacking shops. Why on earth did I do so little to prepare for my own dream?

Looking back, I can see that I did most of the planning on my own, not involving my partner much. Maybe I figured I needed to catch up. Perhaps I was burdened with a warped feeling of gratefulness, considering he invited me to share his dream: "Here dog; eat my scraps." Maybe the work of thinking through a shared experience was too hard and I foolishly thought it would be easier to just blunder ahead rather than talk it through ahead of time.

How pathetic am I?

We talked about hiking together on Assateague Island, Virginia, as sort of a dry run, but he backed out because he said it was too far a drive from Richmond, where he lived. That would have given us the chance to see how we interact hiking with one another.

I spent more time learning to dry my own beef jerky than in uncovering what my hiking partner was thinking when he invited me to join him. My sister once gave me dating advice: if you always think about your relationship, you do not have much of a relationship. I know I should not dwell on the past or harbor resentment, but all I can think about is how terribly wrong the direction this hike has taken.

We always did fine tossing a football, playing bridge, or getting dinner together at the dining hall, none of which induces stress like starving, carrying heavy packs through monsoons, or swatting mosquitoes and black flies for entertainment. You see a different person emerge when the acid drip of stress begins.

I assumed we would walk near or alongside each other as my father and I did on Assateague. My dad and I did not spend every minute side by side, but we walked close enough so we could talk when we felt like it, even in single file. We could call out something of interest such as a hawk flying overhead or the foundations of abandoned buildings overgrown with weeds and vines. Each night we lit a fire on the beach and talked or just stared into the flames. We may have been silent at those times but we were together.

I flew to Maine to live someone else's dream. There are so many things in my life that make me happy, so many things I love to do. I enjoy reading history which is why I wanted to spend a semester amidst the castles of Europe. I enjoy public policy and have volunteered on political campaigns and might have spent this summer interning in Washington, maybe even working on Capitol Hill. I love playing baseball but instead I have sentenced myself to a summer away from the diamond and the batter's box. Instead of choosing to pursue one of my many passions, I went along with someone else's. As what? His convenient helper? His Sherpa?

My life has been a journey wandering without a map and

without blazes to follow. No sooner did someone offer a direction than I followed it, leading me further from where I need to be. "To thine own self be true," Polonius said to his son. I realize now that I am not a hiker guy: I am a ball playing, movie going, book reading, and sightseeing guy. I do not seek endless tranquility; I long for engagement with other people. I admire the beauty of nature but not to the exclusion of everything else I consider beautiful.

The Trail, especially for those who hike alone, offers seclusion most of all. After leaving the Sabbath Day Lean-to, I hiked over the Bemis mountain range, walking in a trance, oblivious to time and distance. All I noticed was the haunting, four-note call of the White-Throated Sparrow. Some people call The Appalachian Trail "The Long Green Tunnel" — I call it that myself. Most of the time, the view from the Trail, surrounded as it is by trees and bushes, is no different than hiking through the Wissahickon woods near my home in Philadelphia. There are beautiful views but most of the Trail looks the same. The long green tunnel means more than just overhanging bushes and trees, though; when we walk, we walk in a tunnel of our own making.

On some days, like this one hiking over Bemis, the tunnel turns from green to grey. Apparently, I walked several miles along open ledges with hidden views of Mooselookmeguntic Lake. I would not know. I could see no farther in the open than I could in the forest. I was walking in a tunnel: a tunnel of clouds.

I knew hiking the Trail would be strenuous, challenging, and difficult. I was warned that boredom would plague me from days on end walking within the tunnel. Yet, there are so many other feelings that caught me unprepared, like how the stress of hunger and fatigue could so quickly destroy a friendship. (Someday, when I am thinking about getting married, I will take my fiancé to Maine. If she can handle the mud, mosquitoes, and rain with grace and humor, she could probably handle the stress a relationship with me would inevitably entail.)

I left without saying goodbye to my partner and he did not as much as grunt toward me. I started my walk dwelling on the fight last night — the accusations, the complaints, and the bitterness. My resentment and anger peaked but finally subsided when I began to explain to myself what caused our flare-up. I was never so hungry that I would fight over who carried the peanut butter, but I never hiked two-hundred thirty miles in the Maine woods. By the time we met at the Elephant Mountain Lean-to, he had reached the same conclusion. Neither of us would yield in the heat of an argument, no matter what the other said. I guess we needed time to think things rationally, to process what was going on.

We took turns apologizing to each other and then walked away from the lean-to, filled as it was with other hikers, to discuss not our problems but our solutions. I carried an empty plastic Gerry tube — so why not fill it with peanut butter? That way we can both munch at will. When we reach our next town, Gorham, New Hampshire, we will buy the mutual goods together and split the cost. After that, we could separately satisfy our personal whims. There is no reason, after all, why we needed to stick puritanically to the food we prepared. A piece of cheese or a bag of cookies might very well be the highlight of a day's hike.

We agreed to share everything in our packs including what was left of the fudge until we reached Gorham. At first we were angry, then we communicated but solved nothing. Nothing unless the shouting picked the logs jammed between our ears. Communication is nothing unless the problems get solved. So hike with a guy or gal — or even a dog — but when you hike with hunger, expect to feel miserable.

JUNE 23, PM

Fry Brook Lean-to

This will be our last lean-to. From here on, I will write from "shelters," the same three-sided structures, but as they are maintained by the Appalachian Mountain Club rather than the Maine Appalachian Trail Club, they go under a different name. As Howard Cosell would say, "Thank you, Danderoo. You add a new dimension to trivia."

I walked behind a porcupine today. Talk about your big, lumbering animal. I did not try to hurry it along as I could not recall whether they could or could not shoot their quills and I was not about to take any chances.

Most of the day I was thinking about the type of world I want to live in. I want to live in a world of honor, where a man's word is his bond. That way, any misunderstandings would be resolved by a question and then an answer, trusted implicitly. For example:

"Did you intend to share that fudge, sir?"

"Who, sir?"

"You, sir."

"Me sir? Of course, sir. Just as soon as I have tried it myself."

Without honor and respect we must either grab what we can or accept that our needs will come last, that we will have to bow our heads in subservience to someone who is more aggressive.

Two countries, suspicious of the other, knowing that responding to an attack means exposing its people to harm, will each attack first because it is less destructive to fight on the other's territory. It is like a piece of fudge. If there is a tin to divide evenly, then the person not carrying it would wish to split it on the first day and not the second, when splitting the spoils means splitting what little remains. I will use fudge for all my analogies from now on.

If I am hiking the Trail to find myself, to jumpstart my life into a forward direction, then what should I do when I have reached that mental mountain peak? Do I stop hiking? When does the act of hiking become an act of selfishness? Where is the end of my journey, when the Trail runs out or when I am ready to move on? A tin of fudge also runs out and pretty darn quick too.

I find myself walking in a daze, the tunnel of my own making, often thinking about doing different things with my life. I was a medical doctor today. I have thought of myself as

a builder and also as a trial lawyer. Other times I think about the world, about people at war or people trying to figure out how to get along. Having the time to dream is like recharging a battery.

Although I believe in hard work, I hope when I am done hiking I will still take the time to dream and not fill every waking moment with so much activity that I lack the time to let thoughts dance in my head. Dreaming by day is different from dreaming at night. For one thing, these dreams are easier to remember and write down. Once on paper, I can find them so I can go back to them, whereas I have difficulty recalling my night dreams. I hope I do not leave these dreams on the Trail; if that is the case, then all they would have been good for was to idle away the miles and the hours.

Dreams are but the first step. Doing something with them is the challenge. Sort of like finishing three quarters the fudge during one day's hike.

JUNE 24, AM

Fry Brook Lean-to

I am writing from a lean-to again, not the shelter I promised yesterday. I share the lean-to with five others and a huge golden dog. We slept side-by-side with one, me, sleeping across the front of the lean-to, exposing me to the early light, which explains why I am writing at 5:30 AM. I am writing next to this Golden Retriever named Lance, who got up to keep me company.

Each of the last few days ended late, allowing little time for writing. We hiked eighteen miles yesterday finishing at 7:30. One way to break this 9 AM to 7:30 PM routine would be to start earlier. I awoke today at 5:10, used the latrine, and then lit the stove to heat a meal of granola with extra chunks of dried apple.

Yesterday's eighteen mile hike started off easy; the whole section was gentle with no climbs of any consequence. It was the first sunny day in a week and today, so far, looks to be our nicest day yet. I spent the last week wearing wet clothing, including wet socks, which prevents my blisters from healing. I hope the washing I gave my feet last night along with another day of dry hiking will result in a step closer toward a recovered body.

Despite the weather, yesterday was not my day. Early in the day I ripped my nylon rain chaps — the sky was still threatening — while crossing through fallen trees. Then, I lost my tee shirt which hung on my clothes drier. I searched for a while, but finding nothing, I chalked up the loss to the same fate which consumed two pairs of socks, a pair of sock liners, and my canteen. It is a good thing my head is attached to my body.

I know I should not tempt fate, but I have designed a great addition to my equipment: a pocket that would Velcro onto my shoulder strap. I could use it to hold my trail guide or a map and maybe the compass. That way, when I want to check my whereabouts, I would not have to take off my pack.

Two days ago we hiked from Sabbath Day Pond Lean-to to the Elephant Mountain Lean-to through wet clouds, yet I remained oblivious to time and distance. No longer was I hiking to get from one site to the other; I was just doing what I was doing, without concern over time or distance. I was neither enjoying the hike nor suffering from it. My eyes were open but I was not necessarily paying attention to what I was seeing and certainly did not track how far I walked. I was living unconsciously.

Walking all day every day helps me become attuned to the clock of nature. When I first left Baxter Park, a mother ruffed grouse chased me away from her nest. As the miles passed, other mother hens chased me while a half-dozen little grouses (grice?) scurried in the other direction. Then the chicks turned into plump miniatures of their mothers all running across the path trying to draw me away from their nest. Further into the month, a mother grouse took flight along with a half-dozen other grouse of the same size. Finally, today, I surprised a lone ruffed grouse.

That grouse was in easy reach of my walking stick. I really have a hankering for fried chicken, crispy on the outside with juices running down my face and over my hands. I just want to bathe in fried chicken juice. I also want to eat ice cream. I imagine warm peaches in rich vanilla ice cream, just soft enough to swallow in big gulps and yet still fall under the definition of ice cream. Fried chicken with an ice cream chaser. I want the whole meal served by a waitress wearing a white apron and a white waitress cap. I want her to smile at me. She doesn't have to do anything untoward, just bring the fried chicken and ice cream — and a lot of iced tea.

I guess I was not feeling so constantly hungry before Stratton because I was still burning my city fat. But after hiking in the Bigelows, I have emptied what was left of my reserves.

I eat so ravenously that the pots are clean before I wash them. When planning our menus, I followed the Third Law of Thermodynamics, which states that matter can neither be created nor destroyed. If I burn a pound of fat climbing a mountain, I would need to eat the equivalent number of calories to maintain my weight. Since I would be burning more calories than I would in my normal life, I anticipated eating more calories per day. I planned menus to provide for this increase, yet, I am always hungry, which explains why I have become so fatigued. My legs keep expanding but my upper body, which is usually solid from working out, has shrunk and I am losing arm and chest strength. I thought the hike would get me into the best shape of my life but I look like a Tyrannosaurus Rex.

JUNE 24

Grafton Notch Lean-to

I guessed wrong on the last lean-to. This one is the last; tomorrow I will be writing from a "shelter." The reason for the slip up was that I did not plan to stay in Grafton after finishing the Bald Plates.

We are less than five miles to the next lean-to, or, finally, "shelter," but getting there requires climbing Old Speck Mountain, which will take six hours. I better get to Gorham, New Hampshire, by Sunday or I will run out of food. I can buy dinner Sunday, then buy groceries and pick up our food box from the Gorham Post Office Monday morning. But getting to Gorham by Sunday depended on climbing Old Speck today, a prospect that became increasingly bleak as the day wore on.

The Bald Plates were just that — bald plates of granite. The view from the top was magnificent, enabling us to see the Presidential Range to the west and Saddleback to the east. As usual, the descent was treacherous and, due to my chafed ankles, painful. There were too many rocks to use my patented "fly down" technique," so with every step I needed to resist gravity, jamming my toes against the front of my leather boots and straining my ankles to keep from falling over. By resting the rest of this afternoon I hope to recover my strength for the long day tomorrow.

JUNE 25

Grafton Notch Lean-to

"Don't drink downstream from a moose." — Words of Wisdom

Grafton Notch again? Once more I write from a lean-to, the same Grafton Notch Lean-to as yesterday, without ever having seen Grafton Notch.

Let me explain. I delayed here because I have spent the past day walking back and forth to the latrine. (My last drink must have come downstream from a moose.) I am unable to hold down foods of any nature, solid or liquid, and have reached the point where illness and hunger tear at me from opposite directions. If I regain my health tomorrow, I will climb Old Speck. If I remain as I am, I will hitch a ride to Bethel, a town eighteen miles from here to find a doctor. My stomach bloats with gas and its contents spew from both directions. My partner has attended me like a true friend, giving me tea or soup as my state of health permits. He said he needed an extra day of rest, since he gets to spend some time reading, relaxing, and recovering.

This illness has sapped what was left of my energy. Meanwhile, the general store in Gorham keeps getting further away than the two long days of difficult hiking I originally expected.

JUNE 26

Speck Pond Shelter

Finally, a shelter.

There are twelve people here watching the streaming drops of water roll off the roof. The crowd includes a father and daughter hiking team and four kids from the town of Sacco, Maine, who were just hiking for a few days through the Mahoosics. The shelter is long enough to sleep twelve across although it is not very deep and a wooden post breaks the floor space in the middle. The latrine crawls with maggots and the spring is a quarter-mile off.

It took over six hours to climb the 4.8 miles from the last lean-to to this, the first shelter. I am still weak from not eating yesterday and still feel queasy. If it were not for the six Pepto-Bismol tablets Steve Jackson gave me, I probably would still be rolling on the floor of Grafton Lean-to.

We shared Grafton Lean-to with different people for the two nights we stayed there, but two of them gave up a day of hiking just to keep an eye on me. They each started at Baxter State Park before us but did not meet until Ken's Hostel in Monson. Steve and Al found kindred spirits in each other. They are vegetarians who carry tamari sauce, carrots, radishes, and whole grains. Due to the weather, neither climbed Katahdin. They spent a week near Stratton staying at the summer home of a country music star, then skipped the Sugarloaf-Saddleback range, rejoining the Trail at Fry Brook Lean-to where we first met them. Perhaps we will not run out of food now thanks to the bag of cream of wheat Steve gave us.

My partner and I prepared Shepherd's Pie for dinner. Steve

and Al ate stir-fried vegetables with lily blossoms. Lance ate some of what he carried in his saddle bags. Steve and Al have supplemented their meals with what they have found along the Trail.

After dinner, we sat around the camp fire and told stories; this is what I had in mind when I signed up for this trek. When the talk turned to what each wanted in the next town, I slipped into a catatonic chant of "Sarah Lee banana cake, Sarah Lee Banana Cake, SARAH LEE BANANA CAKE." It brought several of them to tears.

Steve and Al told us about Steve Jackson, whom they heard about from a ranger. Apparently, in 1975, a fellow named Doyle hiked the entire Appalachian Trail in 66½ days carrying just a day bag. His father drove ahead in a Winnebago leaving caches of food at the lean-tos. Steve Jackson has set out to break that mark without assistance. I would not bet against this man.

By the time Steve Jackson arrived last night at the Grafton Notch Lean-to most of us had already dozed off. But climbing mountains in the rain after dark can be risky; we all woke to find out who the newcomer was. While he unpacked his small bag and made dinner, he told us his story. He was less than two weeks south of Katahdin (it has taken us four). Although he did not have anyone waiting for him in a Winnebago, he does not carry much in the way of gear: no sleeping bag, no tent, no stove. Although Jackson carries his own gear, he said his bag rarely exceeds twenty five pounds, less than half my bag. Traveling forty miles *a day* cuts down on the number of days between food pickups; plus he eats at the diners and small town restaurants along the way.

What type of man is Steve Jackson? Thin and wiry, with a

high mountain-folk voice, he projects enormous amounts of energy channeled towards his single-minded goal. He said to us, "I'm hiking the Trail to get in shape . . . ."

(I thought people got in shape for hiking the Trail, not by hiking it.)

. . . for the first solo expedition across the Arctic Circle."

He was dead serious. This has been his dream since he was sixteen and now that he has figured out what he needs to do, he will work single-mindedly to make his dream happen. He said he will finance the trip through the publication of a novel called "Operation Winter Storm," about the conquest of the world by the Fourth Reich, a feat accomplished by the destruction of twenty-one American cities using nuclear devices similar to the type expostulated in the senior thesis of some Princeton grad. For some reason, the US would blame the Soviets and would retaliate by bombing their major cities crippling both countries. Then the Fourth Reich will roll in and take over. Okay then.

On his eighteen foot Arctic sled Steve will build a "space capsule made from foam, wood, and a proprietary Air Force plastic." He will store provisions in the capsule by day and then empty the sled each night to sleep. He will cook his food using either solar heat or a hand generated stove.

"I'll take along some freeze-dried food, although most of the sleigh will be filled with dog food. I'll live off caribou for as long as I can. When that runs out I'll eat the freeze-dried food. When that runs out, I'll eat my dogs, one — by — one."

The trip will take four months to cross the pole. He hopes to end up near a Soviet Arctic missile installation at which time he expects to be picked up — immediately.

By the time any of us awoke, Steve Jackson was gone on his

way to achieve records for events as yet unimagined. He left me with the example of man's unlimited capability to fulfill his dreams. He also left me with six Pepto-Bismol tablets.

We were also visited last night by another distinguished guest: the first Northbounder, Andy Carter. Andy comes from Plains, Virginia, and is no relation — so he said — to Jimmy Carter of Plains, Georgia. We all listened to his advice on where to get good eats and what to avoid. He told us to make sure we save room for the unlimited buffets at Dartmouth College and the Graymoor Monastery, and to make sure to stay at the home of the Washington Mountain Mystery Woman. He said that we will come upon two women nurses dubbed, "The Snail Sisters."

At every lean-to, we read the Trail Registers for information and warnings from people who have hiked before us. But it is odd that people like Al and Steve knew about Steve Jackson who left after them and that Andy knew about the Snail Sisters, who also started after him. There is a buzz that somehow transmits messages up and down the Appalachian Trail, like drums along the Mohawk.

Andy gave us a stern warning about what lay in store for us tomorrow, saying "It was some of the toughest hiking I have faced" — and he is almost done.

JUNE 27

Carlo Col Shelter

"Become the person your dog thinks you are."
— Words of Wisdom

One mile left and then no more Maine. Good bye to the land of mud, black flies, sores, and sickness.

With us at Carlo Col are Steve, Al and Lance, Helen and Pat, and one of the Sacco kids. The other three quit before seeing the Notch, taking a side trail to hitch back to where they started. The rest of us walked through the Notch together, helping one another up, over, and under the massive rocks. There was real camaraderie today, something I have missed thus far on the trek. Hiking within close proximity of others, getting the chance to know people, and finishing the day with a campfire. Now, if only I could get some use out of that left handed zipper.

I spent a lot of time talking with Steve and Al. They are several years older, putting their formative years squarely in the Sixties. Steve has long hair and a beard. Of course it has been a month since I last shaved or cut my hair, but Steve sported this look all year round. But the best companion of all was Al's dog, Lance, a large golden retriever, not the washed-out blonde type, but one that radiates gold when the sun hits his fur.

Al rescued Lance when he was a puppy. Someone bought him then gave him up. If giving up a dog would be less painful than giving up your child, you should not own a dog. But then again, a lot of people make crappy parents too.

I asked why he named him Lance. It turned out that this is short for Lancelot. "He's an unfixed male," Al said, "so he lances-a-lot."

Although I first met them at the Frye Brook Lean-to, it was not until we spent the past two days walking through the Mahoosics, that I really got to know them. Although they foretold the coming of Steve Jackson, they provided a contrast to him, and for that matter, to the two of us.

Steve is pretty sure he is the first Southbounder to leave Baxter State Park this year. Al also left two weeks before us, but we caught up because they spent a week outside Stratton.

When I limped to the Grafton Notch Lean-to, the others were already sitting around a fire, talking about concerts and their experience on the Trail. The first to greet me was Lance, who came over as I entered the camp and escorted me to where the others sat. When I asked my partner if he would mind stopping for the night, everyone cheered, as they had agreed to continue hiking if I was willing to push on, but every one of them was hurting and worn from the steep descent from the Bald Plates.

Rand told the others that when I planned a destination — in this case the top of the next mountain, Old Speck — I pushed to reach it, no matter what the time, no matter what the effort. This was strange of him to say because he usually arrived at these destinations first, with me dragging up the rear as I did so on that day.

Steve and Al, however, were different.

They did not begin the day with a destination in mind. They hiked together and when they felt like stopping, they stopped. I told people I was hiking the Appalachian Trail. Steve and Al explained that they were hiking *on* the Appalachian Trail. When I told them I refused offers of car rides along the five mile stretch of road leading into Caratunk, they shook their heads with pity. Not that I enjoyed the walk. The road passed through a section of houses, some old and beautiful, others not much to look at. But walking on a hard paved road with a heavy backpack on damp gritty socks sears the undersides of my feet like breakfast sausage on a griddle. But since I hiked every inch of the

Trail thus far, I was not about to cheat my place in history just to reach Caratunk. Steve and Al, on the other hand, skipped the unpleasant parts like the road leading into Caratunk and a couple of mountains for that matter, and they intended to keep skipping the unpleasant parts for as long they chose to hike.

"I'm not hiking to get my name in a record book," Al said, "I don't even care if I reach Springer Mountain."

I almost fell into the fire when he said that. How would he possibly reach Springer Mountain if he does not care? With me, it is the goal of reaching the end that keeps my legs moving. Without the goal of reaching Springer, why am I doing this? Without being a legitimate Thruhiker, this is just a hike. And if all I am doing is hiking, who cares how far or how long I go? Yet in contrast to Steve Jackson, who cares not about hiking but of records, I wondered on which side of the table I really sat.

After spending the day throwing up, I recovered enough to hike. I moved slowly and was the last hiker to arrive at Speck Pond Shelter. Although I plodded up the steep mountain, I felt better at the end of the day than I did at the beginning. If not for Lance, who hung back from the others to accompany me, as if herding a sick calf, I might not have reached the shelter at all.

A teacher at my high school annoyed me by declaring that animals, like dogs, lacked intelligence. His point was that writing sonnets defined intelligence, whereas a dog reacted to basic stimuli like hunger. Spoken like someone who never shared life with a dog.

A dog displays a different type of intelligence, that's all. In fact, while we are at it, not all people write sonnets, but does that mean they do not possess intelligence in their own way? If I were stranded in the Amazon, would I be better off with a high school English teacher or an illiterate native tribesman?

Lance and I enjoyed our Kodak moment at an overlook looking north and west. In the distance we could see rocky outcroppings on distant mountains and the afternoon sun glancing off lakes — but mostly we saw the tops of trees. From our height we could see the horizon, for no mountain appeared higher than where we sat. I pulled a piece of Logan Bread from the plastic bag and smeared peanut butter on it, cutting off a few chunks for Lance to eat.

"Careful," I told him. "That's the densest, drying substance known to man."

For the most part he was content to lie down next to me while I gazed over Maine; other times he sat up and lay his head on my leg. As I stroked his head, I talked quietly to him.

He looked at me with so steady a gaze, I felt unnerved. I wanted to let him know how much I had suffered from this hike, that I was hungry, cold, weak, wet, and sore. But he travelled those same miles, so there was no point complaining. I wanted to tell him about the on-again, off-again relationship with my partner, but he would know nothing about harboring resentment or dwelling on anger. I wanted to tell him how I felt uncertain about my future; he rested his head on my leg and sighed, as if to tell me that worrying was the problem, not my lack of direction. We gazed over the wilderness from where we had travelled but he knew nothing about dwelling on his past.

Eight of us, including Lance, climbed across the Mahoosucs,

the last mountain range in Maine, and the steepest climb north of the Nantahalahs in North Carolina. By climbing Old Speck one day, and leaving the rest of the Mahoosucs for the next, we made the journey a bit easier. Even Lance needed help hiking through the famed Mahoosuc Notch, where pieces of rock had peeled off the steep sides of the mountains, filling the Notch with stony debris of enormous proportions.

There was one point where I lifted Lance to Al sitting on top of a rock wall, who then lowered him to Steve who was waiting on the other side. We climbed over small boulders and under huge ones, sometimes dropping our packs through jagged rock mouths and sliding through on our backs or stomachs. The wind blew chilled air from under the largest boulders where ice survived the summer's heat. It took us an hour to traverse the mile long canyon. Every turn faced us with new challenges, either a rock wall to climb or a boulder to crawl over or under: it was the Rubik's Cube of hikes. And all the time we heard the call of the White-Throated Sparrow.

We ended our hike at the Carlo Col shelter just one mile short of the border. We were so close to leaving Maine but the next shelter was five miles away and none of us had the energy to push forward. Plus, if we did, that would put us so close to Gorham, we would have to wait until the town opened to get our post office delivery of food. This means we will reach New Hampshire two days late. For so long, I awoke each morning with the thought that I was a step closer to leaving Maine. I guess I will have to wait another day.

JUNE 28

Gorham, New Hampshire: Free at Last

I have been clicking my heels together saying, "There's no place like New Hampshire. There's no place like New Hampshire." Twenty-eight days of rain, mosquitoes, mud, moose moo, and hunger, nary a switchback nor a bridge — and somehow I survived to tell about it.

There; that wasn't so bad.

We left Carlo Col for the town of Gorham, the "Gateway to the White Mountains." I read that it was a charming Victorian town but I could care little for charm. I wanted banana cake. I wanted ice cream. I wanted a long, hot shower. But then we came upon a flier wrapped in plastic that told us that due to a trail change the distance to Gorham now lay seven miles farther than the distance stated in the guidebook. Steve and Al said, "Why worry? If you want to go to Gorham, go to Gorham. The AMC changed the Trail this year, which means the Thruhikers in years past went the shorter route." But I faced a quandary. I had hiked every inch of the Trail thus far despite blisters and bruised ankles. Could I deviate from the one true Trail just because of Sarah Lee Banana Cake?

My partner saw my confusion and said he would go along with whatever I decided, but was suffering from a massive Big Mac attack. I looked again at the mountains of New Hampshire. How rugged they looked. After twenty-eight days of Maine, with rain soaking us on twenty-four of them, I could wait no longer. "To Gorham," I said, "By the quickest route possible."

Imagine four people happily walking along a road, accompanied by a dog. The Wizard of Oz? Nope. But I was so delirious to have left Maine I felt like skipping. As soon as we reached the center of Gorham, Rand and I found a rooming house with a shower for five dollars each, and then doubled back to hit the McDonald's we passed. Steve and Al were already seated when we brought over our trays piled with Big Mac's, fries, and shakes. Whereas our friends ate only shakes and fries, Lance knocked off six hamburgers, so he made his contribution to the "Billions and Billions."

Steve and Al were not staying in Gorham but were hitching south to catch a Dizzy Gillespie-Dave Brubeck concert. We said our goodbyes to the two bearded backpackers and the one furry one. Lance put his paws on my shoulder and looked me in the eye. Then, he got down, turned, and went with Steve and Al down the road leading out of town. I will miss them.

Gorham is a quaint New England town. Many of the houses are of wood, painted in pleasing shades of blue, yellow, and green. This satisfied a need for me, the longing to be in a real town with real people. Across the street from the guesthouse is the town park. During the afternoon, two uniformed teams played a softball game. At night, lights flashed, music played, as a carnival attracted the Gorham young.

After *Mickey Dee's*, we found a store with a frozen food cabinet. My partner bought a half gallon of vanilla peach ice cream and I bought that long awaited tin of Sarah Lee's Banana Cake. Not being a trained dietician, I cannot attest whether this was the healthiest of meals, but the two of us knocked off both in one sitting.

Alas, that was the end of the joy we would find in Gorham. The old woman who runs the rooming house reeked of mistrust and insisted we pay her in advance. She warned us not to get any water on the bathroom floor, as she had just paid to repair the linoleum floor and fix the ceiling in the room below. Well, that was great news. The one thing she did not do was leave the shower curtain long enough to reach the edge of the tub nor did she provide towels that could actually dry our bodies let alone the big pools of standing water on her bathroom floor.

So, how was I supposed to take my shower? As soon as I turned the water on, it sprayed on the floor. Many shower curtains turn black with mildew where they come in contact with the tub. This is why they should be left out of the tub to dry. Some, like this genius, cut the bottom of the curtain to eliminate the part that gets mildewed, which is also the part that keeps the water from spraying out of the tub.

When I saw the puddle, I turned off the shower and tried to dry the floor on my hands and knees — naked — using the one small towel she gave us. Needless to say, she will not be adding our names to her Christmas card list.

JUNE 29

Imp Shelter, New Hampshire

It is 10:00 PM and we have just finished dinner. It is very dark in here but my candle lantern lights the page well enough to write.

And what a dinner it was. Tuna stroganoff, rolls with strawberry preserves, brownies for dessert, all washed down with a bottle of wine — under the aforementioned candlelight. Hiking without all the others, we were again living in our own separate worlds. Again I left first; again he passed me without a word. When we reach our destinations, we both do what has to be done, one makes the meal while the other pitches the tent or gathers wood or water: we are very efficient that way. But it seems strange that we do not discuss the hike or anything else for that matter.

The wind whips past this shelter so ferociously it creates music as the air whistles through the cracks. Even inside its holder, my candle flickers, chasing shadows against the wall. Fortunately Imp Shelter is a cabin and not a lean-to, so it provides protection from most of the wind. Otherwise, staying in a lean-to perched on this bluff 3500 feet up, we would have to spend a chilled and miserable night sitting in the dark, as even the glass enclosure around the candle lantern would not keep its flame lit.

The shelter reminds me of the epic poem, *"The Cremation of Sam Magee,"* which my father would read to us before bed along with other poems like *"Gunga Din," "Casey At The Bat,"* and *"If."* In fact, most of what I would call my morality was shaped by these poems. From *"The Cremation of Sam Magee,"* I learned to never go back on a promise and, consequently, take care not to promise much. Sam was from Georgia, the land of peaches and ice cream, but up in the Klondike, he was slowly freezing to death so he made his friend promise that should he die, his friend would cremate him. Well, Sam did die and his friend was unnerved over burning his friend, but honor insisted that "A promise made is a debt unpaid." And that explains why I am sitting in a windswept shelter in New Hampshire.

The name of the shelter brings back memories of that good old school, the University of Virginia. One of the many quirks of The University are the words and symbols one sees painted on its walls and steps. These are the secret societies, such as the Seven Society, which paints large "7"s on walls with an infinity symbol above the number. There is also the IMP Society, which stands for "Incarnate Memories Persist," meaning that the genius of Thomas Jefferson still guides the University of Virginia. Since these are secret societies, the rules of membership state that you cannot reveal whether you are a member. But since the Honor System at UVA does not permit lying, cheating or stealing, this creates a dilemma. When asked point blank whether you are a member of a secret society, you may not reveal the truth but you may not lie, so you would have to stand and leave the room — "Can't lie; can't reply." This is all hearsay, of course, as no one has thought to ask me to join a secret society — or not?

JUNE 30

Somewhere on the Carter Range

We almost had ourselves a situation.

The "Croo" (the localized spelling for the crew of people working at the White Mountain Hut System) at the Carter Notch Hut told us we would not be permitted to camp on the Presidential Range because of the danger of sudden storms. Even during the summer, a blizzard could sweep the treeless ridge, ripping at our tent with grizzly ferocity — and even that supposes we would find space between the rocks to pitch a tent. The summit has earned its name "The Rock Pile" because it has no dirt, no trees — just heaps of large rocks. The distance across is fourteen miles. Moreover, it will take us twelve miles tomorrow with a monster climb just to reach the top of Mt. Madison, the northernmost peak of the Presidentials. So to clear the range, we will have to hike twenty-six miles with a four thousand foot climb. Our prospects for tomorrow, the first day of July, look grim.

I came upon the Croo swimming in the crystal clear Carter Lake at the base of the towering mountain called White Carter Dome. My partner was sitting on a rock off to the side, not talking with anyone, just enjoying the sun with his pack off.

When they saw there were two of us, it clicked that we were Thruhikers. They asked about our trek thus far and gave us our only two options for camping on the Presidential Ridge. We could wander off the ridge a half mile to the tree line to pitch camp or we could camp before reaching the top of Mt. Madison. Either way, we would camp on the side of one of the highest mountains in the northeast United States. I could picture turning in my sleep and rolling down to Pinkham Notch. One of the Croo warned that we better not even think about spending the night near any of the White Mountain Huts. These beautiful mountain lodges cost a lot of money and no "Croo" Chief would want the atmosphere spoiled by a couple of squatters in red and blue sleeping bags. "He might come after you with a shotgun," he admonished. We then learned that he was the "Croo" Chief at Carter Notch Hut — a wonderful guy with a great sense of humor once we assured him that we planned on moving on.

Mt. Carter faces, but is not yet part of, the Presidential Range (Get it: Carter? Jimmy Carter? No?) We climbed the steep slope into the Carter Range and found a bed of spongy moss about fifty feet off the trail, which should make tonight's sleep restful. Although for the most part, we walked along the edge of a steep mountain, there were stretches of flat areas called "Cols" between the peaks. Once we decided to spend the night, I walked off the ridge until I discovered a spring of cold water. I discovered both the spring and the campsite without the guidebook. I just followed my intuition. How cool is that?

JULY 1

Madison Spring Hut

Now that is what I call, "A Mountain." I have just walked down from the peak of Mount Madison, some 5300 feet high, onto the Presidential Range. That was the most difficult climb I will face until we reach Tennessee.

Earlier today, I jumped from ledge to ledge, in my descent from the Carter range into Pinkham Notch. By jumping down the side of the mountain, I spare myself a great deal of pain while all I risk is breaking my neck.

The main lodge for the entire hut system lies in Pinkham Notch. I stopped there long enough to buy some snacks and take a hot shower. That made two showers in the same week — I must be getting soft. While in the shower I heard a guy tell his buddies that he could not go on because he lost the ring clip that attaches his shoulder strap to his pack frame. "You're in luck," I yelled from my shower stall. As soon as my quarter's worth of hot water ended, I jumped out of the stall, fished through my pack, and handed him my extra ring clip which I found lying in the middle of the Trail a ways back. Although I saved this guy's hike, he seemed less than grateful. It occurred to me later that he probably tossed his clip into the toilet to avoid the killer climb into the Presidentials. Some little old ladies just don't want to be helped across the street.

A plaque in Pinkham Lodge lists the people who have died on Mt. Washington. Exposure and rock slides I can understand on the highest mountain in the Northeast United States — but hit by a car? Man and nature collide on Mt. Washington. Not only can the non-hikers drive, they can go by train.

Pinkham Notch lies directly below Mt. Washington. The road to the top leaves from its parking lot, which was crowded with cars. The Appalachian Trail also leaves from the parking lot and crosses the road several times before it winds north along the notch to the base of Mount Madison. I walked along a pleasantly wooded and well maintained path. Yet, despite the modest ascent, my pack belt ripped loose from the frame again, forcing the entire weight of the pack onto my shoulders, just as it did while I was climbing Chairback Mountain. I probably damaged it during my jarring descent into Pinkham Notch, so chalk up another argument against leaping down the side of a mountain.

Not only does the broken belt dump the weight of my heavy pack on my shoulders, it makes climbing dangerous, since the pack shifts with each step. Mountain ledges are bad places to lose one's balance.

I kept walking until I reached Peabody River where I lunched on Logan Bread, peanut butter, an apple, and a bit of the cheese. There I tied the belt to my pack using some nylon rope. Here's an idea: enclose the frame inside the pack, then the transfer of the weight of the pack will not depend on two tiny nylon tabs that keep ripping or onto little circular rings that mysteriously fall off. Furthermore, instead of shaping the frame into flat rectangle, how about shaping it to fit the contour of a human's back? This way the weight of the pack will not shift back and forth while rubbing a hole through to the vertebrae.

Luncheon at The Peabody proved one of the most restorative hours a person could spend. I sat on a large rock in the middle of the river surrounded by rushing water. Where did this water come from? I could recall no rain for several days yet this river gushed down a mountain that ended somewhere in the sky no more than a mile above where I sat. Furthermore, despite its force, the river was clear of silt and debris. Compare this with an urban stream which is brown with silt. I thought about the spongy bed of moss I slept on the night before. If we covered that sponge with asphalt, the water would rush down the mountain as soon as the rain fell rather than soak into the ground. All the water would rush into the stream at the same time, leaving nothing saved for dry weather. The level of the stream would rise and fall with each rain, undercutting the bank, then washing the soil away.

Yeah, that would suck.

A chipmunk hopped to the next boulder looking at me eating my PBJLB — Peanut Butter and Jelly on Logan Bread. I broke off a crumb, careful not to drop it into the water, and placed it near the chippy. "Be careful," I said as he sniffed my offering. "It's the densest, driest substance known to man." But he did not heed my warning. The chippy ate the crumb which immediately began swelling inside him. For the rest of the hour, he just lay on his side watching the river flow.

I was so taken with the beauty of Peabody River that I

thought how great a res-
taurant could do there,
with a terrace over-
looking the cascading
river and a double deck
parking lot in the back
— with trained ducks
in the lobby. Or
maybe a condo-
minium. But what
good is a terrific
view if we destroy the
view? What a conundrum. When we
attempt to provide access to every experience, we kill the very beauty we seek. Moreover,
we would lose a chance at ecstasy if every experience came
easy. If everything came easy, nothing much would matter.

After I finished my lunch I resumed my hike. For three
miles I climbed steadily, stopping only to rest and munch
some gorp. I continued to climb until I passed the timber
line. Above me loomed Mount Madison, all exposed. The
sky was a deep blue without clouds and the sun kept the air
warm even above the timber line. When I reached the first of
several peaks that led to the highest peak, Mt. Madison, I saw
Rand emerge from the timber line below. I could have waited
for him but then he would have left me in his dust. It was not
that I was competing with him but I did not want another
reminder of how much faster he hikes or of how vastly different were our visions of this hike. I wanted to climb Mt.
Madison first; today, at least, he will not zip past me. I hiked
up to the peak without pausing, took a look around at the

world from just under the cloudless sky, and then walked down the well maintained switchbacks that brought me to the Madison Spring Hut. I felt exhausted; I could not make my legs move any further. The thought of bushwhacking off the ridge to find a space to unroll a sleeping bag enervated me further — but I saw no alternative.

I just needed to rest until Rand caught up.

As I approached the Hut, a member of the Madison "Croo" rang the bell for supper. I asked him for some water and a place to wait for my partner — nothing more. But he took one look at me, saw the exhaustion from deep within my eyes, and asked, "You must be the first Southbounder. Why don't you spend the night here? You look like you could use the rest."

It was that easy. When Rand arrived, he looked anxiously at me wondering if I intended to pay the fee as neither of us could afford to stay at these beautiful mountaintop lodges with their great meals, soft bunks, and showers. The Croo Chief came out to meet us and said we could sleep on the dining tables unless a couple of bunks went unclaimed.

After helping the "Croo" wash the dishes we sat with them while they ate their meal and we ate ours. Of course, we would have been rude to turn down their offer of homemade bread or their invitation to try the wonderful stew they prepared with chunks of beef, beans, potatoes, carrots, and onions that, unlike our five-minute meal, cooked for hours in a large cast iron pot. It would have been terribly rude not to trade our meal for theirs — at their insistence — and we are anything but rude — starving, famished, exhausted — but never rude.

After the meal, we witnessed one of life's most spectacular

sights — sunset from the top of the Presidentials. The clouds above us turned pink while those nearer the horizon turned purple. Those closest to the sun turned orange. The sky remained light a while after the sun set. The thirty people spending the night at the hut returned for a brief night of fellowship then bed.

Staying at these huts is not cheap but they are worth the price. The Croo provides three all-you-can-eat meals plus hot water and coffee along with a comfortable bed under a roof and between four walls high above the timberline. The hut system enables people to hike through the Presidentials on the Appalachian Trail and other lesser-known trails without having to carry a pack as heavy as I do. All they need is a light backpack and a water bottle, as the huts take the place of the tent, sleeping bag, food, and stove.

The ingredients for our terrific dinner arrived the same way we did. One of the jobs of the "Croo" is to climb the mountain each day with a pack basket filled with supplies — literally a large wicker basket with shoulder straps. The "Croos" at these huts, the folks who carry the one hundred pound packs up the sides of 5,000 foot mountains, are all the kind of healthy, vibrant, wonderful people I would expect to find. Even though they climb these mountains daily, they treat us like heroes, whereas in reality they are the ones who make the Presidentials accessible without destroying the beauty to reach that goal. I help no one in pursuit of my solitary journey. So, really, who is the hero?

JULY 2

Home on the Range

I went through the entire state of Maine without feeling thirsty. The mountains in New England soaked every drop of rain and snow into their mountain core before releasing their stores to spurt forth into the many springs I enjoyed. Some, the guidebook fussed about, others escaped mention, but they all contained a sweet taste my plastic bottles could not capture. Good water to a thirsty person is the dearest drink of all.

I travelled a long way from that lonely swamp they call Maine. Leaving Madison Hut, after a wonderful breakfast of an egg, cheese, and sausage casserole, I felt full of energy and raring to go. After Madison, the journey to Mt. Washington was simple, just a 900 foot change in elevation peak to peak. To get to Madison, people hike. To get to Washington, most take either a car or a train. You really appreciate a place when you climb over 4,000 feet to get there.

Although Mount Washington gets all the publicity, the picture people see is the entire Presidential range. From Madison, I walked around the peak of Mount Adams, paid homage to the founder of The University of Virginia by climbing Mount Jefferson, skipped Mount Clay — he was not even a President — and then climbed Washington (my favorite President). By the time I got to the peak, the wind velocity reached fifty miles an hour with a wind chill of ten degrees Fahrenheit, according to the weather equipment there. Though I left Madison Hut wearing long pants, I had changed into shorts by Mount Jefferson — I walk faster in shorts — but by Washington, I wished I still wore the wool pants.

One does not feel lonely atop Washington; there are several buildings, a parking lot, and a railroad station. The first sign I saw was "Wall Drugs" nailed to the side of the building that houses both a restaurant and a gift shop, but the squat structure itself looks like something one would find at an Arctic outpost. I have never been to Wall Drugs in South Dakota, but some day I will go there for my free ice water. Wall Drugs, the Grand Canyon, and the top of Mt. Washington are destinations people visit, stay for an hour or less, buy souvenirs, and then leave for the next place on their list.

The visitor shop was too crowded for me after the laid back atmosphere of the Madison Hut. After leaving, I passed a group of people huddled around a woman lying on the ground suffering from hyperthermia. Wearing shorts, and surmising I could add little to what the crowd was doing (primarily blocking the wind, I guess) and not wanting to join her as a victim, I moved on.

A lot of people feel development spoils the natural beauty of a mountain — especially one that took a day and a half to climb. In a Trail register on Bigelow Mountain, one Northbounder from last year complained about a few wood and dirt steps that were built on the path leading up the side of the mountain. "Why don't you just put an auto road up here so you can rape this mountain, just like you did to Mount Washington and Clingman's Dome?"

I liked being able to escape the freezing cold of a hot summer day — and relished the climb over some food and drink. I also would not want to dig a latrine on "*The Rock Pile.*" The train and the auto road open the top of the world to people who could never reach it on their own, although as I saw, not everyone comes prepared. Although the people who drove to the top hold different views of adventure, we both share a common desire to stand atop the highest peak in Northeast United States. Moreover, if there ever comes a day when the forces for unrestrained development threaten natural places like the Presidentials, it would take a larger constituency than just a few scraggly Thruhikers to prevent this from happening. Sometimes you have to let others join you inside the tent.

JULY 4

Morning, About 4 Miles West of Route 302

This makes the second night in a row that we camped by the side of the Trail. We slept under the shelter of spruce trees, enjoying the peaceful melody of a brook.

Back at Christmas, I met a woman at a party at my next door neighbors. When I told her what I was about to do, she told me to include her on the journey in any way I could as she lives in New Hampshire. After some thought, I got back to her asking her to meet us at the junction of the Appalachian Trail and Route 302 at noon on July 3. After six months, we arrived fifteen minutes late. (We will have to pick up our pace.) Mrs. Thomas was on hand to meet us, the first familiar face — well, at least, a face I had seen once before — since leaving for Maine.

When we started this morning, Rand asked what I thought we would do with the Thomases. I told him we would have to play it by ear and see what happens; we still were six miles and several thousand feet of climbing away from Route 302; plus I had my doubts they would show.

She volunteered to greet two strangers with a box of food thirty-five miles from her house. Yet, she never discussed these plans with her husband. When I called from the top of Mt. Washington, I could hear him in the background, first alarmed, then upset. I was forced to listen as he tried to discourage her, talking about time lost working on the house and the wasted gas. I really did not want to hear a lesson on how married people should discuss their plans in advance. I guess I would feel upset too if my wife made a commitment two months earlier without letting me in on the secret. They could use some communication tips from the two of us.

I mailed the box of food in May so I needed to hang in there until they resolved their dispute. Nevertheless, they not only showed, they brought the peanut butter and margarine I requested in my last postcard. We paid her for the peanut butter and margarine then put these important staples into their respective containers, winding up with extra peanut butter. Mrs. Thomas offered to buy it back, but two Appalachian Trail hikers seldom worry about excess food. We devoured the remainder right in front of her. She then suggested we might be interested in a "chocolate bloopity-bloop." We said yes without knowing what it was she was talking about.

We drove to The Willey House, five minutes down the road in Crawford Notch — a tourist trap since the 1800's — which sells ice cream among other touristy things. The mixers for milkshakes were broken, so we all ordered ice cream cones. I also bought four slices of bread for PB&Js — a little kid's sandwich I have grown to enjoy even more as I have gotten

older. Then, after finishing our cones, we got back into the car and returned to the Trail, where, to my surprise, they hiked with us for two miles, before taking a side trail that would bring them back to their car. Mr. Thomas said, "Since we came all this way, we may as well make the most of it." Atta way kid.

I have to say that the whole rendezvous gave me the willies, an expression that was created in honor of the Willey family, whose premonition the creek would rise in the storm caused them to abandon their house, only to be crushed in a rock slide that knocked everything down to the left and right of their house but left it standing. I can't make this stuff up.

I kept thinking about what I might have done wrong. I did not troll the party looking for people to run errands but her offer meant that we did not have to carry as many days' food out of Gorham. When I planned the food drops, I figured we would enjoy seeing people along the way more than calling for general delivery at a post office. We will see my parents in

Vermont for the next one, then the one after that from Didi Osgood, who lived in the same dorm as we did, although a year later. I am grateful to Mrs. Thomas and could not reasonably have expected more — like maybe a picnic lunch of fried chicken, potato salad — maybe some beer or wine — but she did offer that chocolate bloopity-bloop.

JULY 4, PM

Troubled Days

Last night, I pitched our tent in a fine drizzle which would later turn into a steady rain. My partner did not think it would rain hard enough to justify pitching the tent so he sat while I pitched it. I told him it would rain, but then again, he told me that if I pitched the tent that close to the side of the Trail, we would be told to move it. He was right on that front so that should have made us even.

We began today with a bad morning. We quarreled over how much margarine to use on our pancakes, although I have already forgotten who wanted to use more and who wanted to use less. The day before, we passed eight Northbounders who made us feel like the beginners we still are. They also made me wonder what hiking alone, but within the general proximity of six other people, would have been like. If we went on this hike separately, I would have left Springer Mountain last semester with the rest of those hikers in March, because taking off the spring semester of my second year would have made more sense for me than missing the first semester of my third year. My partner needed a class that was taught only in the spring and, after all, this was his dream. If I had left Georgia in March, then at least my image of spending nights around the campfire with my fellow hikers would have turned true. Yet I am heading south, not north, and the only person going my way is at the same time too many people and not enough.

Ever since that first day, when we stopped to gape at that blowdown, we hiked apart — sometimes far apart. When he would catch up to me (I left first almost every day) I would quicken my pace but he would still blow by me. Once in front, he would leave me in his dust. (Of course, this is metaphoric — it rained too much to raise dust in Maine.) As a result, he usually reached the destination, then waited for me, feeling put out about fitting into someone else's plan, giving up a more scenic view he passed or maybe would find in a few miles. If we hiked within chatting distance, like Steve and Al, we could make these decisions together. Refusing to hike within close proximity meant we could not change our plans.

We met on the first day of college. George, from downstairs, stuck his head in my suite and called "anyone for basketball meet at the courts." I yelled I would play and went into my room to get ready. I put on a pair of thin inner socks then slipped on my athletic socks. Then I put a Doctor Scholl's foot pad into each of my Adidas high tops and laced them tight. When I got out to the asphalt basketball court I met some of my dorm mates. One of them, who would one day ask me to hike the Trail, was playing barefoot — on asphalt. I was hiking the Trail with a Centaur — half man, half goat.

The miles wore on. Sometimes, when he arrived at a campsite long after me, I worried. And of course one time he did not show up at all. Nothing irritated him more like having someone worry about him in the middle of nowhere. One of the reasons he hiked was to leave all worries — and worriers — behind.

We say words to each other but we never communicate. We never said, "This is how I feel when you do this," something I read we should do. Instead, we blame each other for the way we feel or we do not talk with each other at all.

What do I know about him? We never talked about each other's past. I knew he lived as an only child, raised by a triumvirate consisting of a mother, a grandmother, and an aunt but I never asked him why. With no brothers or sisters, he got used to spending time alone. I never asked how growing up as he did made him feel or whether it shaped who he is, positively or negatively. Although I am tempted to connect the dots and reach my conclusions, I might be missing some important connectors along the way.

At school he focused on physics and astronomy, endeavors that favor the more solitary thinker. He is two inches shorter than me but he is every bit as athletic, with a hard, lean body. He is uniquely equipped, physically and emotionally, to hike the Appalachian Trail — alone; what I do not understand is why he asked me to hike with him nor do I understand why I accepted.

He visited my family in Philadelphia before we left for Maine and saw a glimpse of my upbringing. I grew up with two sisters and a brother. For our family vacations we crowded into a station wagon, with the youngest one loaded in the back like a suitcase. My dad's rule was that we all ate dinner each night as a family. We could do whatever we wanted after school, so long as we were sitting at the dinner table by six — and we would never think about missing Friday night dinner, when he would pick up my grandmother on his way home from work.

Do not pity me; family dinner was no obligation; it was fun. Our conversations were raucous, each wanting to get the attention of our father. Family was the cadence of our lives. We would talk about school, sports, politics, art, literature, civics, history. We finished each other's sentences and changed the topic back and forth. We performed, we told jokes — anything to make our father laugh or show his pride through his hazel eyes. Eating dinner in silence and spending all day, every day, alone was not something I planned on, since I never anticipated committing a capital offense.

And what about me at school? Although both of us were Echols Scholars, a special program that meant we did not have to declare an actual major or worry about prerequisites, he declared as a physics and astronomy major whereas I joined the Political and Social Thought program; not a real major, but a program that offered great cocktail parties. Up until then, I took courses from just about every department at The University.

We could not have been more different.

I guess I am learning through this hiking experience that unless you enjoy being surprised, hurt, or disappointed, it pays to take a deep dive into the history of the person you will spend time with before venturing on a long walk — or on any relationship for that matter. We all come complete with a personal history. Although we may break from our past on occasion, we tend to settle back into the patterns we have known. I like noise; he likes quiet. I like spontaneity;

he likes order. We don't complete each other, we annoy each other. I should have learned more about him and he should have known more about me. We talked about communication but we did not know what to communicate about, at least not about anything that mattered.

One of my favorite memories of family vacations was of the nights spent around the picnic table playing pinochle in the light cast by the Coleman lantern. Pinochle was the only card game we played as a family and we did it more to spend time together, to laugh and talk, than for the game itself. Now, my nights consist of eating dinner, cleaning up, then either reading or writing in solitude.

During our first year in college, Rand and I played a lot of bridge and we formed a good team. We could fall back on that now; all we need are two other hikers to get a card game going. And I guess we also need a pack of cards.

Since my partner and I are chained to each other by my stove, his tent, and our food, we have to plan in advance where to meet each night, which robs us of the freedom a Thruhiker ought to feel. Maybe if I hiked the Trail with a female classmate, we would want to hike within each other's sight. We would choose our campsites through collaboration not acquiescence. We would end each day's hike in each other's arms. We would watch those spectacular views, like that blowdown, holding hands and whispering our awe to each other.

I suppose we each imagined the hike but neither of us could put that vision into enough words to share it. Now the frustration of so wildly missing the mark has made us physically sick and sick of each other. Since hiking together caused him trouble, we hiked apart. But instead of freedom; it robbed the hike of spontaneity. We hike alone in the woods but we do not feel free — how weird is that?

We would rather keep walking than show the first sign of weakness by wanting to wrap up early. Or, we reach our destination burning with resentment for having walked past the loveliest of views. After hiking alone all day we greet the other with a muffled, "Huh," and then sit under a tree, bemoaning the loneliness, wishing we had someone to talk with.

We camped on July 2 at the base of Mt. Jackson overlooking a brook with a pool deep enough for a swim. I could not have imagined a more beautiful spot, but with no one around to share my joy, it was pointless to say, "Wow, what a beautiful spot." Why bother? We laid our sleeping bags on the sandy ground and fell asleep listening to the breeze rustling through the spruces.

So after arguing about margarine one day and about the tent on the next, we started the 4th of July disagreeing how to pursue the day's hike. We agreed upon our destination, fourteen miles away. The hike started with a three mile gentle rise along an abandoned railroad grade. The Trail then doubled around to form a horseshoe which, we learned from a Northbounder, one could slice by taking the side trail across the valley then up the steep side of the ridge. I argued that whereas it made sense for the Northbounder to hike down the steep side and across the valley, we would be walking across the valley and up the steep side of the mountain. Rand was all for the shortcut, saying "I don't want anything to do with that boring old railroad grade."

Actually it was not all that boring. I left first, without specifying which route I would take, but figuring that I would have a long enough jump on him that I could take the railroad grade — the true Trail — and still beat him to the junction. But I stopped at the Zealand Falls Hut along the way to chat with the Croo and then I took some time to look at the waterfall before reaching the junction at the top of the ridge. There I sat on a rock for a while enjoying the view while eating an orange. I never enjoy a hot dog as much as when I am at a baseball game and I never enjoy an orange as much as when I can look out from the top of a mountain.

There was a definite logic to my argument in favor of the railroad grade. For one thing, it was the gradual climb I predicted. Walking up a ramp may require more steps than climbing a staircase, but the latter requires far more energy. That is why gyms offer both Stairmasters and treadmills, but we all know the Stairmasters are for those wanting the more grueling workout. Besides, with "The Method," I barely sweat from walking up an incline anymore.

I realized while walking what my second point was in favor of following the true Trail. Taking shortcuts are like taking drugs, an addiction once started is not easily stopped. We abandoned the Trail to get into Gorham; perhaps we could be forgiven because the route we took was the actual Trail last year. But taking a shortcut for the sake of a short-cut undermines our status as true Thruhikers. Next people will claim to have hiked the Trail because they stood atop Springer Mountain and Katahdin but skipped everything in between.

Regardless of the soundness of my argument, the strain of the past few days has thrown all logic aside. If I argued for the short cut, he might have argued for the horseshoe trail. We have slipped into the slippery slope of emotions, but I am caught in the same dynamic and am not clever enough to see my way out of it.

We are both factual guys — we look for facts not emotions to support our arguments — and, normally, he comes across as the far more Vulcan-like than me. But of late, we seem to argue from emotion first, then seek facts to bolster our point of view, the opposite of what one would expect from the two of us: Eagle Scouts, Echols Scholars, and friends.

From where I ate my orange, the Presidentials stretched northeast, looking every bit as powerful as they did the first time I saw them from their northern side. Here it is, the Fourth of July, the day we honor those same men — Washington, Jefferson, Adams — who risked their freedoms, their fortunes, and their lives because they longed for a new way of treating people with respect.

For over a month I have looked at this country and am ready to render judgment: it is beautiful. But that is not the America we celebrate today. Other countries have natural beauty. What we honor today is a love of freedom that intertwines with our national consciousness. We respect the freedom of others, regardless of how they wish to live their lives, so long as they in turn respect the freedoms of others. That is what we are about. Pray to your god, read your books, think your thoughts, speak your mind — just do not infringe upon those same rights.

We believe in the political embodiment of the most simple of moral philosophies: "Do unto others as you would have them do unto you." Rarely has this been practiced. Instead human history has witnessed a succession of one person climbing on the backs of others. The good news is that it has nothing to do with race. In a room full of White Christians, the right handers will try to rule over the left handers, or vice versa. Black tribes in Africa annihilate other Black tribes because of what distinction, I do not know — certainly not skin color.

What is it good for? The tendency to elevate and denigrate seems embedded in the human condition. It takes a conscious effort to resist this tendency. We once were bent on destroying each other with spears and tomorrow it will be death rays; technology only makes us more dangerous. The founders of this country, following what they believed were the natural rights of mankind, tried to rise above the chaos. Jefferson listed three values: Life, Liberty, and the Pursuit of Happiness. We do not condone the taking of a life; we do not impose our way of life on others; and we do not judge others by what gives them happiness, so long as they are not preventing the life, liberty, and happiness of others. Everything else is commentary.

We have to get past discrediting the nation's vision because some of the founders owned slaves. The problem was not with the vision but how the Founders limited access to that vision. We have struggled since, at great cost and turmoil, to remove those limitations. Because of that continuous struggle each generation can claim a part of this nation's founding.

After my orange, I continued walking through the scrub pines that filled the ridge-top forest. The path was smooth and the slope gentle. I walked with a bit of a jazz tune playing in my head, helped along by the sole that was separating from my right boot, giving my steps a bit of a back beat, bit-of-a-back beat, bit-of-a-back beat. The warm breeze whistled

through the trees
and rustled the
leaves. There were
springs trickling
into glens, adding to
the music I heard
all around me. Moss
and wildflowers grew
along both sides
of the trail and when
the trees swayed, rays of

sunlight illuminated these otherwise subdued colors so
that they would shine green and white and yellow along the
path. I stopped to watch a red tail hawk circling on the warm
updrafts, the sun turning its tail feathers an iridescent red.

I figured that since my partner had not blown by me, he
must have passed the junction already but would wait at
Galehead Hut according to plan. From there we would head
to the Garfield Ridge Shelter to spend the night — legally —
near the summit of Mt. Garfield. What I did not know was
that even as I stood at the overlook, Rand was at Galehead
telling people he was worried because he left after me but
had not seen me all day.

I took a sip of water from my water bottle and munched
some gorp. A hiker heading north approached me. "Are you
David?" he asked.

I stared into his face but did not recognize him. "Do I
know you?"

"No. Get your pack on and don't stop hiking until you
reach the next hut. Your friend is worried sick about you and

the rangers are about to organize a search party right this minute."

Throwing on my pack, I walked as fast as I could to Galehead Hut. I was greeted with a chorus of "Where have you been?" but all I could answer was, "Enjoying the view."

Sharing equipment was one thing, but worries? That was more than either of us bargained for. I felt foolish causing trouble, trouble that occurred because my partner took this moment to become "worried sick" about me. The obvious answer was I stayed on the one true Trail. As I stood there, watching as the needless and unwanted concern of strangers turned to disgust, I could not help but wonder, "How much longer can we continue to hike together when we had not hiked together at all?"

CHAPTER FOUR

Love

JULY 6

Lost River Shelter, Kinsman Notch

I have not been able to write of late as both of the last two days ended late. I barely have time now considering how I devoted an hour repairing my right boot, which has lately gone for the flapper look. This I repaired by boring two holes through the toe of the Vibram sole using the awl function of my pocket knife and then passing a nylon cord through the holes, around the toe, and then through the bottom eyelets.

Today was not one to hurry through. Under a beautiful cloudless sky and especially along the cascading Eliza Brook I walked for hours in a constant state of enjoyment. New Hampshire has been delightful and although each of the past eight days has been strenuous I have not felt pain, thus leaving my mind free of unpleasant thoughts. At the end of a long climb here in New Hampshire, there is unfailingly a ridge offering wide views of the surrounding area. Unlike Maine, where my thoughts were divided between food and leaving Maine, in New Hampshire, my thoughts have generally centered on my family.

(There, that's better. I just lit a candle; no more cursing the darkness.)

I thought about my father who has spent his life fighting injustice. He used to read to us *Gunga Din* by Rudyard Kipling, in a dramatic style, his voice thundering for emphasis, *"Din, Din, Din"* — rhyming with "green, green, green" — the closest he ever came to singing. Someone not acquainted with the poem might dismiss the story as some white colonialist talking about his superiority over the dark skinned water carrier. But that would certainly show a misreading of the poem, the same way someone who watched one episode of *"All in the Family"* might have taken away the message that it promoted bigotry rather than cast a mirror to it. The soldier concludes that Gunga Din is "a better man" than he is, with more character, more loyalty and more courage — a surprising confession for an Englishman who spent his life believing that superiority of character was somehow correlated to skin color. My father's philosophy was that a man should be measured not by the color of his skin, but by the substance of his character.

Our house was always visited by people of different colors and faiths. My parents lived in Japan during the Korean War, not long after the global victory over "the yellow peril" and when they came home, my parents co-chaired the US-Nisei Friendship Society at a time when the memories of Pearl Harbor were fresh and it was not obvious the Japanese would later become among our country's closest allies. The Nisei were Americans of Japanese ancestry whose allegiance our country questioned during World War II, stripping them of the rights Jefferson promised those who believe in America.

We were close friends with Indians, Chinese, Catholics, Blacks, and Jews. We lived in a neighborhood that never reached the point at which it flipped from all-White to all-Black. In contrast, just a few miles from my house, entire neighborhoods changed from White to Black in just a few years.

A seesaw can move from up to down with very little weight added to it. At first nothing happens, but then just a small amount of extra weight causes the seesaw to change positions completely.

When a Black family moves onto an all-White block, most of the people will greet the newcomers, but it only takes one White family to react based on race to put their house up for sale. Should that house sell to another Black family, most of the neighbors will again welcome the new family but someone else would put their house on the market because, although one Black family might be acceptable, two certainly were not. But this gradual shift is not sustainable. By the third or fourth house, the block reaches the point of no return and the entire block goes up for sale and changes completely.

Whenever too much product comes to market at once, the price falls. Then the issue is no longer just racial prejudice but economic as well. In most neighborhoods, the house represents a large portion of a family's assets; the threat of declining home values offsets the desire for friendliness. As one block heard of how another block's values collapsed, the number of houses necessary to reach the point of no return shrunk to one. Nobody wanted to see years of home value wiped away overnight. Nor do they wish to live in a neighborhood with the same social problems — the same crime and disrepair — that caused the first Black families to leave their previous houses.

One of the many bad outcomes from *White Flight* is that all the first Blacks wanted was to provide a better school and community for their children. They wanted to live the American Dream. They worked, perhaps were veterans, and they valued education as the path to advancement. When the Whites took one look at them and cleared out, they made it easier for people to move in who did not share the same values and ambitions. Instead of welcoming families who wanted to share the American dream, the Whites threw them back over the wall, not only robbing them of the value they had just paid for their new houses but reducing Black advancement to "moving from a smaller ghetto to a larger one," as Martin Luther King said.

Unabated, people will act in their best interest. My father tried to change these dynamics by getting the "next" White family to stay. He and others of like mind (like my mother) met the challenge of the Sixties and Seventies by increasing their involvement in the social structures of our community like the West Mt. Airy Neighbors Association along with so many like-minded who people rallied around this community. My Dad served as president of the Home and School Association and my Mom ran the hoagie concession at the school fair. He was the Boy Scout leader and she led the Girl Scouts. They were not going down without a fight.

My parents found committed partners among Black families, like the onomatopoeic Vivian and Donald Black. Mr. Black could calm a storm and all who knew him loved him. If I had grown up in a segregated community, he would never have influenced someone who looked like me, and I may never have been influenced by someone who looked like him, nor would I have known Otto Atkins, my bugling merit badge counselor, or Miss Irene Randleman, my fifth grade teacher who helped me hit my stride academically. If Blacks are inferior, a viewpoint held by both Whites and Blacks (unfortunately), then how could these people have made such a positive impact on my life? An integrated community not only enables Black kids to identify with the American Dream, it teaches White kids how to live with people who look and act different: a powerful tool for dealing with a complex world.

Are we better when we insist that Black people pretend they are White to get ahead? Or is our country improved when Blacks despair of finding their place in our society, only to retreat to the defeatist and angry culture of the ghetto? The third way, the promise of the American Dream, means that we accept each other's culture as the ingredients of a better tasting stew. We would never want Italians to leave behind their music, their festivals, and certainly not their food. Nor do we ask that of the Irish or the Chinese. Different cultures can embrace the American dream, and that means Blacks can too. Fitting into our country is about beliefs, not skin color, not language, not the way we celebrate. America is an ideolgy, not a race.

We have a giant stew but there is a broth that binds us together. It is a belief that every one of us has the freedom to reach our potential, to search and find what makes us happy. It is the respect for another's individuality. It is the willingness to fight for another person's right to be a free.

My father held that belief as his basic tenet. He did not

judge by religion or color. He wanted to build a society in which all people could celebrate Jefferson's words: life, liberty and the pursuit of happiness (although attaining happiness is up to the individual.).

When my father ran an organization, part of his role, as he saw it, was to find successors. He said a true leader was not someone who ran the organization but who could inspire successors to carry on. He made sure the positions of responsibility went to those most capable and not just to the people he knew the longest or with whom he shared an identifiable trait. He integrated new blood and new ideas into these organizations. He taught that the real work was never just about the Boy Scouts or the school fair — it was about the community. Without a stable community, none of these other activities could last. Community organizations bind a neighborhood together; without them, we live in a bunch of houses. If a vibrant community was the goal, then racial identities would not matter. We would all be standing on the same side of the barricade. He knew that when people worked alongside each other, they would learn to trust each other and build friendships. No more panicking and packing.

Our neighborhood, West Mt. Airy, became more integrated during this time, but it never reached the same crisis point as other neighborhoods. The Black families that moved onto our particular block were people of great character — an Anglican minister, an army colonel, and a doctor, each one married to beautiful, elegant women, with children who were well-mannered, well-educated, and motivated to get ahead. They were smart, hardworking, responsible members of our community. If the White people could not judge them by their character, well, the disgrace rested entirely on the

Whites. But no one fled from our block. Houses opened up when older people downsized; some Whites moved on the block during this time as well.

My Dad was tough, fearless, and he held a vision of a world in which people would look past their differences to find the common ground. He was a liberal because he wanted society to change but no one should mistake that for being a soft touch. He never once shrunk from the intimidation of radicals like the Black Panthers. He never overlooked criminal behavior. One of his expressions was, "All it takes for evil to triumph is for good men to do nothing." He was an ideologue; his ideology was America.

In 1968, when hope was murdered on a motel balcony in Memphis, our city, Philadelphia, like many others, burned overnight, and what were once poor areas became blighted. The city I will visit when I reach Pennsylvania has vast areas that are not safe for either Whites or Blacks. We defeated dictators to save democracy, but we cannot save the cities in our own country.

Four years ago, two guys from the Hill Gang jumped me when I was coming home from school. When my father came home and saw my black eye, he told me to get in the car and drove around trying to find them. The Black families we knew would have ridden in that car with him if he had asked.

Maybe some Blacks would have excused an unprovoked attack on a White kid; because they felt alienated; because something once happened to them or to their ancestors; whatever. When it is not your kid getting beat up, it is easy to shrug and say "Boys will be boys." Of course, that tone changes fast when a White boy strikes back at a Black boy — then it is racism. Where does it all lead? Violence never stops at the first victim. Overlooking harmful behavior in a community creates a callousness towards the use of violence. Ignoring this behavior rarely causes it to go away; fostering violence sinks us into a more brutal world.

We will not live in the world we want unless all of us stop excusing our group from harming others. It is not who got the beating that matters, not if we want the beatings to stop. For our communities to recover, people of all colors and faiths need to link arm and arm to put an end to the depravity, the violence, and the destruction that should have no place in American society. *"All it takes for evil to triumph is for good men to do nothing."* If you want to live in a world in which your kids feel safe, then you must stand up for the safety of all kids, not just your own.

My father used to speak each year at various gatherings held in mostly Black schools and community centers for Martin Luther King Day. He told me that after one such talk, he tossed out, "And if anyone wants to shake the hand of the man who shook the hand of Martin Luther King; I will be standing in the back." It was a throwaway comment; he didn't think much of it. But to the mostly Black audience, it was spiritual. Every person in the audience stood and, without a word, waited in line for their turn to shake his hand.

The divide is not so great; it is only as wide as an out-stretched hand. Most people, Black or White, want to live in a world in which they can get paid for the value they produce, earn the opportunity to succeed based on their effort and ability, and to raise children who can go further.

We often hear we are all the same under the surface of our skin but we are more similar than that. What are we but chemicals mixed together, some carbon, some hydrogen, some nitrogen? What are those molecules of chemicals but combinations of atoms, which themselves are comprised of atomic matter. We are all just rearrangements of the same basic stuff.

Where do we differ? Mostly in our beliefs and attitudes. We learn from our parents, our community, our peers, schools, churches, and media to want, to hate, to care, and to love. Where we go wrong is that we do not understand America enough to love it wholeheartedly. Instead, we let other voices confuse our minds. Viet Nam, slavery, segregation, discrimination, sexism; these are caused by people, not the American Dream. What is the Dream? It is not a house with a lawn and a car in the driveway; it is about beliefs. Certainly, the American Dream is not about the men who started this country, it is the ideas that matter.

That is what my father stands for.

JULY 7

Wachipauka Pond

I put an end to the White Mountains today, going up and over Mount Moosilauke. Afterwards, I hitched to Warren, the closest town with a store. Now here I am sitting in front of a fire by the pond, sipping hot chocolate. I am leaning against a tree, looking across a pond that stretches so far I would call it a lake, if it were up to me. I can see no other person, not even the slightest hint of another human being. (This is odd considering I am hiking with someone.) I feel refreshed after my dip in Wachipauka Pond.

It got hot today, but not muggy, and whatever sweat and dirt that once covered me is now part of the pond. Today's

walk was tough enough to be challenging yet short enough to leave time and energy for other pursuits. Today I am a dog: no worries, no pain worth mentioning, no smoldering resentments to ponder; just me enjoying the air, the sky, the dry path, and the trees.

Tomorrow looks to be one of those days when we will walk to exhaustion, then camp, not knowing where until we get there. Our goal is to reach Hanover, New Hampshire, in two days. We will then target Gifford State Forest in Vermont two days after that, crossing seventy-six spirited miles over the next four days. I heard from a Northbounder that Steve Jackson walked from Glenncliff to five miles past Hanover in one day, well over forty miles. I am afraid I am going to lose that race.

I met this guy in April who warned that, what he called "The Long, Green Tunnel," would grow monotonous and I would soon conclude hiking it would become a waste of time. "Not everyone," he said, "is cut out to spend that much time hiking." I am not normally good at following advice, so most people do not offer me any. Yet, I have a nagging suspicion he may be right. I have been at this for well over a month and have not reached the end of the second state, for goodness sake, and I now find myself racing from one rendezvous to another.

I did not follow advice well when I started college either. My program did not require me to take prerequisites, so I skipped them, starting with a first semester filled with upper level courses, as if the laws of time and effort did not apply to me. I took an upper level psychology course thinking I would read the introductory textbook during my spare time. I sat through the first day of an upper level class on foreign policy with Scott Nance, a friend from my dorm. The professor announced this was his first class as a professor, then rattled off at an unintelligible pace. After five minutes, Scott closed his notebook and said, "Well, I'm out of here." Since I am not a quitter, I stuck it out and got a "C" for my efforts. I hate to quit. As the great Willie Mays said, "Quitters never win and winners never quit." Nearly two years later, I cannot recall a single point I learned in that class whereas Scott has just been accepted into the Government Honors program. I am such a dope.

At least on the Trail I have learned to follow guidebooks and the blazes left by others who have trod before me. Hiking the Trail has shown me that not only can I grow by placing one foot in front of another but also that there is a lot to learn from the people who have walked before me. There are plenty of trail registers with sage words of advice. Most of the good things I have going on this trek are due to advanced preparation learned at the feet of others. Maybe I should try doing this in my real life?

We hiked Katahdin without packs and then limited our first week to ten miles a day. In those early days we were training for the rest of the hike. Ideally, we should have gone home to redesign our food supply to come closer to actually meeting our nutritional needs. Even with supplements such as Sarah Lee Banana Cake, tins of fudge, and bottles of beer, our regular diet of Bisquick, macaroni, and instant potatoes has not kept us healthy. Again, some advice and better planning would have made the hike more enjoyable.

Rand and I created a lot of the recipes back at The Anchorage, the house we lived in second year. When we made our first biscuits from a box of Bisquick, we stirred it completely to make sure we got rid of all the lumps. When the biscuits came out of the oven as little shiny inedible disks, one of our housemates, Steve Redding, ran off with one. A few minutes later, we heard hammering at the front door. Steve ran a cord through the biscuit, hung it on the nail and wrote "knock here" on it. We learned not to stir the batter so much.

So, what can I do to carry these lessons forward? I certainly can improve my skills. I am a poor writer; my one writing course in college proved that. Not only did my teacher stick me with a "D-" she added the gratuitously cruel comment, "Your writing has gotten worse as the semester progressed."

I used to blame my high school for my poor writing because the teachers emphasized multiple choice tests over essays. I see now how I made the choice to remain a poor writer. I wrote quick and easy papers in English classes, received disappointing grades, and concluded I lacked the talent; I figured it was a right brain, left brain kind of thing. Like hiking long distances carrying heavy packs, writing is a journey that begins one step at a time.

A few months ago, I visited my aunt in New York. I told her that one day I would become a writer. She scoffed at the idea saying, "You a writer? You haven't suffered enough to become a writer."

"Guess what? I hiked through Maine. How about that for suffering?"

Maybe I lack the genius to become the next Shakespeare, but not everyone who writes a book has to be Shakespeare. Just because I may not become a concert pianist, does that mean I could never enjoy playing the piano? I can hike the

Trail without being Steve Jackson. I have caught myself saying, "Sure, if I were the runner he is, I would get up early enough to run before classes too." I am now embarrassed to admit that I alone have placed limits on my life. One thing the Trail has taught me is that if I do not do it for myself, no one will do it for me. I am responsible for my happiness and success. And I may as well start now.

I have dreams but dreams alone will not get me out of my sleeping bag. I have to will myself awake, will myself to walk, will myself to climb when my body aches. In my confusion, I have drifted through life, an easy follower of another person's dreams. From now on, I will seek advice and wisdom to better form my own dream but I will not go around looking for others to come up with a dream for me. And when I find my dream, I will pursue it to the ends of the earth, regardless of what others might say, with the same purpose and will that has carried me over these mountains.

JULY 8

Mount Cube Lean-to

I passed a Northbounder today bringing my unofficial count to fourteen. There have not been any women included in that count, although, it cannot be much longer before my path crosses that of Pam Nelson, with whom I have a dinner date.

Pam wrote in the March issue of the Appalachian Trail News saying that she would be leaving Springer Mountain on May 7 and was looking for people to hike all or part of the Trail with her. I wrote to her saying that although I could not hike with her, leaving as I was from Mount Kathadin, I would be interested in joining her for dinner sometime in July. "I'll wear something blue."

To this she wrote saying, "This is the strangest dinner date I have ever accepted, but see you then."

Was she referring to me when she used the phrase "strangest dinner date" or just the event? Well, anyway, I wish her the best of luck and hope she does go all the way — at least as far as New Hampshire.

I hiked fourteen miles today with a steep climb up Mount Cube to make the day seem longer than the actual mileage. It also rained all day — our first completely rainy day since Maine. Regardless of today's weather, New Hampshire has been great, so much better than Maine. Besides physically being more attractive, I have found the people to be nicer, the drivers more willing to pick up hitchhikers, the weather finer, and the girls prettier. In fact, I do not think I shall ever cross the Maine-New Hampshire border again.

The Northbounder told me to "prepare for the feast of your life." He also told me to look out for the Snail Sisters and make sure to spend the night at the October Mountain Lean-to in Massachusetts. I have heard all this before from other hikers and in the Trail Registers. Still, I am excited to stop at Dartmouth for the meal of a lifetime and cannot wait to meet the Snail Sisters, those two sexy nurses who are hiking the Trail in high heels, white skirts, and tight blouses, wearing their stethoscopes around their necks. The Northbounder did not describe them but I have a pretty good picture in my mind.

Hanover, New Hampshire. Thayer Hall

Bloated! Stuffed — how else can I describe the relentless pressure thrusting my stomach outward, preventing me from sitting upright in my chair. When I finally got to a place where all my needs could be met, I overindulged.

I first heard of this delicious all-you-can-eat buffet from Andy Carter, the first Northbounder we encountered when we shared the Grafton Notch Lean-to with him and Steve Jackson. Since Andy, all of the now fifteen Northbounders enjoined us not to miss Thayer Hall. "The White Mountains? Yeah, they're okay if you like mountains, but let me tell you about the food at Thayer Hall." I, for one, came prepared to dine, feast, and gorge. My last meal, aside from a few cookies, was breakfast. I did not even eat gorp in anticipation for tonight's meal. The buffet of chicken and pasta dishes may seem tame to the connoisseur, but any meal piled high with meat, mashed potatoes and gravy, fresh milk, rolls and butter, and ice cream would have me dreaming about for days. As filled as I feel now, I cannot wait for the breakfast buffet tomorrow.

As I sat writing, and waiting for my body to adjust, a Dartmouth student tried to sell me a junior class t-shirt. I told him: "Right class, wrong school." When I told him I came from old Virginia, he asked me if I knew his girlfriend.

"Strange," I said, "but I thought she was my fraternity brother's girlfriend." Oops! Did I say that out loud?

He spent the next twenty minutes telling me how much he still loved her, how beautiful she was, and how crushed

the "Dear John" letter left him. Finally, I bought a shirt so he would let me digest my food in peace. It will replace the one lying in some puddle in Maine.

Dartmouth has a great campus, full of lively music, smiling faces, and lovely young coeds. There is something about a college town, wherever it is, that breaths vitality.

In the spring, I was walking past the Corner where a lot of the shops are at the University of Virginia, when a student started singing, "Hey, good looking. Whatcha' got cooking… Oh!

"Don't stop," I said.

"I'm sorry. I'm not wearing my glasses — I thought you were someone else."

"You thought I was George, didn't you?"

"Yes!! How did you know?"

I have known George since my first day of school and he was my roommate during my second year. We both have brown wavy hair and mustaches so if you are nearsighted, you might get us confused.

So, here is what I thought about today. It is a brilliant strategy for attracting more girls. I realize it is rather convoluted, but I am a chess player at heart.

As a back story, I went to Central, the all-boy high school in Philadelphia. Central is the second oldest public high school in the country. Every so often a student from Girls High, the all-girl school a very long block away, took a class offered only at our school; usually in a foreign language. In a scene reminiscent of another Central High School, boys would line up on both sides of the hall chanting their appreciation for the brave young lady who walked the gauntlet.

Young guys know what they want, they just haven't figured out a subtle way of asking for it.

As I walked around Dartmouth today, every girl looked attractive to me. Scarcity makes the object of our desires dearer. The problem I have been facing at school, thanks to George Gerachis, is that there seemed to be two of us. To make matters worse, we took the same classes, we roomed together, and we ate together. Our effect on women was plentitude, not scarcity. I realize that I need to get rid of George.

Bear with me.

One of the guys in my first year suite grew up near me. He is as handsome, as funny, as creative, and as intelligent a person as you will ever meet. In fact, he is far more handsome than I, far funnier, more creative, and far and away more intelligent.

He suggested that when we went home over spring break, we should go out for a double date. He took a girl from his church to a restaurant called The Black Banana for dinner. After dinner, I joined him with my date for a show and then to Winston's for some of its famous onion soup.

When we arrived back to school a week later, Time Magazine broke a story about the voice of the Gay Student Hotline. Some state legislators wanted the young man thrown in jail because — stay with me on this — he was also paid as a resident advisor. Since Virginia is a state school, he was technically a state employee. The Commonwealth of Virginia has a law on its books prohibiting sodomy. Since this guy is the voice of the Gay Student Hotline, and therefore safe to assume he is a homosexual, he therefore must be a public tax dollar receiving sodomite. I did not instantly make the connection because I did not know what a sodomite was, so that is something else I learned in college.

Since no one has come forth with proof that he practices sodomy, he agreed to give the Hotline to someone else. That someone else turned out to be my friend from the double date.

There is a spinoff effect to celebrity; all of a sudden people were asking me about it. What did I know? When did I know? My friend who could have gotten any girl he wanted, voluntarily removed himself from the dating pool. How did that harm me? I just moved up a notch. What's wrong with that? So my plan is to get George to start digging guys, then I will get the girls singing to me.

After Hanover, my next goal is Gifford State Park in Vermont where I will spend a few days with my parents. I could use the break, as both big toes have become infected, my right boot is falling apart, my back hurts because of the broken back belt, and I am now barefoot at night since losing my moccasins this morning.

I hate losing things, yet it goes on and on. I remember complimenting myself on the fine job of securing the moccasins to my pack. Later, I do not know why, I felt for them but they were gone. I raced back, but the same game replayed itself: in one corner, you have "me," earnestly seeking to recover my possessions, and in the other corner, you have "me," realizing that each mile spent in search was a mile I would later have to turn around and hike again. Do I go back five miles, making a ten mile roundtrip only to come up short? Suppose the mocs are six miles back? The feelings of inadequacy mount with each mile neglected; the frustration mounts with each mile spent in fruitless search.

I may very well have no clothes left by Massachusetts.

Cloudland Lean-to

You may talk of pizza and beer, when your refrigerator is near, and you watch your TV shows upon the screen. But when you're without a bed, you'll be glad for slices of bread, and perhaps a piece of meat to slip between. (Apologies to Kipling.)

It was hard leaving Dartmouth but the Trail must go on. After a wonderful breakfast, we hiked through the eastern part of Vermont, over land flat enough to enable us to make up for lost time. We still have twenty-three miles to hike tomorrow to reach Gifford State Park, where my parents await.

We have spent several days racing to arrive on the same day as my parents. We made this more difficult because of our even greater need to reach Thayer Hall in time for dinner. This left us with an awkward fifteen miles today and twenty-three tomorrow — that is just how the lean-tos fall on this section of the Trail. We hiked only eight miles yesterday into Dartmouth, so that was a waste of a day; if they would have located Dartmouth a few more miles south, these days would have evened out.

Long before the mind can dream of luxuries, the stomach yearns for necessities. I guess because I lived on Logan bread and water, my dreams in Maine were filled with visions of fried chicken and Sarah Lee Banana Cake. Back home, where those necessities were in abundance, my mind would turn to other things: I thought about sex every fourteen seconds. But on the Trail, hunger and fatigue drive the opposite sex off the top forty play list of my mind.

I sometimes wonder about my morals. Am I free and easy or am I shackled by inhibitions? With the exception of hiking through Maine, I do very little to hurt my body. I don't smoke, I don't take drugs — in fact, I don't even drink coffee. Someone once said, "So you'll live to be a hundred, but who calls that living?"

I would never lump sex in with drugs. Sex is a biological necessity, whereas drugs are artificial dependencies. Certainly the Bible found no harm in sex; everyone was getting to know each other. But should I even mention religion when talking about modern morality? After all, I am a modern kind of guy, capable of thinking for myself, sensible enough to form my own judgments. Sex is natural and I am all about being natural. This I concluded in the middle of a New Hampshire forest. Fortunately, I wrote my philosophy down; otherwise I would have forgotten it by the time I could put my new natural morality to use.

I think about good and evil a lot these days, but how natural is my thinking? My generation grew up after the Sexual Revolution. We read Playboy Advisor and watched uncensored movies. How much of our morality is natural and how much a reflection of the messages meted out by the external world? Have we emerged beyond the need for the stability of religious morality or have we replaced the lessons from the Bible with those of television?

Born Again Christians require their adherents to reaffirm their faith as adults. Any religion, or political affiliation for that matter, that confidently believes its teachings, should create a re-entry point so people can rejoin based on a conscious choice. Choice becomes reality when we bear the consequences of our decision. Religions that say people have a choice, then hunt them down when they leave the fold, must not have a good story to tell.

Walking through the airport to catch our plane to Maine, we passed several pink robed followers of the Hare Krishna cult. These were not people born in India. Why would a Protestant, Catholic or Jewish kid join the Krishna's? I do not know the psychology behind this but I doubt these kids rejected a strong connection with the religion of their birth. Most likely, they chose to follow this cult or the more extreme versions of their own religion because they lacked moral certainty in their lives. Weeds tend to flourish in untended fields.

My morality is certainly driven by my religious upbringing, in part by my parents, in part by my peers, and thoroughly by the hormones that rage through my body. I envisioned meeting a pretty hiker with whom I could link sleeping bags. I even bought a sleeping bag with a left-handed zipper just for that purpose: "Be Prepared," that's my motto. Then there are those two nurses, the Snail Sisters, walking toward me. Two beautiful nurses wearing form-fitting white uniforms, with fishnet stockings, one a red head and the other a blonde or maybe a brunette, I have not yet decided. I am thinking — Charley's Angels. And those nurse hats, set jauntily on their heads. Don't get me wrong: I am the first person to defend constancy as the basis for love. I just figured that constancy on the Trail would have to end when the sun came up.

Last night, after eating my fill at Thayer Hall, I sat on an overstuffed sofa in the common area of the large house that provided shelter for passing AT hikers. I met a quiet girl there with an understanding smile. I entertained her with some of the old standbys like, "Did you hear the one about the moose . . . ?" We walked around a bit and then wound up in her dorm room, discussing feelings and wants on the edge of her waterbed. I felt dizzy from the proximity, from the long awaited moment. I so hoped she would be gentle. But at nine thirty, just as I was about to make my move, her phone rang. I walked around her room looking at her books and albums. When she hung up the phone, she walked over to me, kissed me on my cheek, and told me what a nice guy I was.

"That was Richard, my boyfriend. He's picking me up, so feel free to listen to my records or crash on my bed if you want, because I'm not coming back tonight."

How not nice, I thought.

I slept alone downstairs on the overstuffed sofa wishing for someone to hold. I finally had enough food; I had shelter; but after a month and a half on the Trail, I wanted more. I wanted the luxuries of life they knew in the Bible.

JULY 12

Gulf Lean-to

The sky is grey; looks like rain. No matter. I will push for these last fifteen miles to Gifford Woods even if it started to snow. This state park has eclipsed Springer Mountain in importance. I suppose that once I make it to Gifford, I will have survived the first quarter of the hike and the rest should be easy.

I left Cloudland Lean-to at dawn and covered eight miles

by breakfast. Right now, I am cooking a gaggle of bacon, blueberry-raspberry pancakes, and pecan twirls. I picked the raspberries but we bought the blueberries, pecan twirls and, of course, the bacon.

A few days ago, before Dartmouth, we found ourselves along a twelve mile stretch between Trapper John Lean-to and Velvet Rocks Lean-to. It was getting late and, since we were walking along a road, we were close enough to confer that we would need to find a place for the night shy of the next lean-to. We were walking single file when a woman in a station wagon pulled into the gravel driveway ahead of us, stopping at her mailbox.

"Pardon me," I said. "But would you know of a place we can pitch our tent for the night?"

I guess we looked pitiful which would explain why she offered her backyard. We never pitched the tent as the sky was clear and the grass provided soft support for our bedrolls.

She took us on a tour of her vegetable patch, handing us a squash, an onion, and some beans to add to our Long Day Stew. Her tomatoes were not large but looked delicious, although not available for me to pick.

I was walking in a dream behind this woman who looked so much like Jennifer O'Neill, the actress who starred in my first R-rated film, "Summer of 42," which I saw when I was fourteen, which was about the same age as the male characters who were spending that summer on Nantucket, where the chief entertainment was imagining the loss of their virginity, not unlike how I spent that corresponding summer. O'Neill played a young bride whose husband goes off to war and hires the boy — me, in my Appalachian Trail fantasy version — to help her with chores such as follow her around the vegetable patch picking squash and beans. In the movie, she learns that her husband was killed in action, has sex with the kid, and then leaves. He dies a lonely embittered man, having never met a woman who could compare. Or maybe he died happy, having that one incomparable night.

I wouldn't know.

JULY 14

Win One for the Gifford

We hiked the last two days across Vermont in a blur, arriving here at the Gifford Woods State Park two nights ago. This park marks the point where the AT connects with The Long Trail and then turns ninety degrees toward the south. A family campground, with camp sites carved out of the forest, Gifford offers me the chance to see my parents.

During the two day forced march across Vermont, I lived with this anxious feeling of having to get somewhere, instead of "living in the moment." Now that I am with them, I feel relaxed — sort of like being home. There is just one touch of awkwardness to this scene. I am here with Rand whom my parents treat like a second son. He, in turn, treats them respectfully, answering their questions and engaging in conversations. So that is where all the conversations were hiding.

This change upset me because he has not shown me this side of him for most of the trip. When I think about it more calmly, I remember that outside of our recent interactions, he and I were good companions, which we would not have been had he been less than a good man. If we were not such good friends, he would not have asked me to join him and I would not have accepted. So something besides being good people made this relationship fall apart.

We have used this hiatus to rest our bodies and to take care of some of the business we need to tend to. We found a shoemaker who will fix the flapping of the sole of my boot. A few days in the shop should also dry them enough to waterproof them again.

Instead of being impressed with my on-the-Trail repair, the shoemaker kept shaking his head muttering, "This won't do; this won't do at all," as if the reason we were in his shop was for him to critique my work. I almost apologized for upsetting his sense of shoe aesthetics.

My mother made the pocket I described out of red nylon with a strip of Velcro on its back. We then used an epoxy glue to put the other side of the Velcro to the pack's shoulder strap. It just may work.

My ankles have swollen so much that I can no longer make out my ankle bone. They do not hurt but my legs feel bloated and look awful. This has reduced me to sitting in a lawn chair for great stretches of time. I am getting a lot of reading in, and now some writing, along with a whole lot of staring into space. Luckily, all these maladies have converged at a place where I can relax, soak my feet, and be mothered.

My mom is a real mother; I mean that in a good way. She feels my pains, fights my battles, and worries about me more than I do, which is nice because I can always say, "Now, mom, don't worry."

So what is going on with my feet? Last year, I ran a five mile race, came home, showered, and then got a ride to

Washington DC. By the time we got to the Smithsonian to meet some other friends, I was completely hobbled. For the last mile of the race, we climbed the steep incline from the bottom of the Wissahickon Valley to the top of the ridge. For a stretch, the ground consisted of soft silt. I thought the mushy treading may have strained my foot, which then could not withstand the marble floors of the National Art Gallery. My friend, Rob Perry, who ran cross-country in high school, suggested taking a supplement of calcium magnesium carbonate $CaMg(CO_3)_2$ commercially sold as Dolomite, because running leaches minerals from the bones. Not having any other answers, I picked some up and by that evening, the pain was gone.

I am like most people. If I knew "An apple a day keeps the doctor away," I would still not eat that apple. One year after that running experience, I set off to hike every day for five months — without the miracle remedy Dolomite. Thankfully, my mother picked up a bottle for me which I transferred to a plastic bag.

She also brought me a large bag of Goldenberg Peanut Chews. "Now who's talking private stash?" She also brought bags of Peanut and regular M&Ms as well as Mounds bars. I gave Rand the Mounds and the regular M&Ms. Shucks.

I could easily eat the bag of Peanut Chews in one sitting. These were invented, according to my father, by his Uncle Lou, who owned a small candy store in the Frankford section of Philadelphia. The Goldenberg's, a rival but more enterprising candy maker, saw promise in the peanut chew so they manufactured, wrapped, and distributed it. The Goldenberg wrapper was the key. When the chicken lays an egg, the rooster climbs on the hen house and lets out a song for all to hear. When the duck lays an egg, the mallard merely quacks and walks away. That is why we eat chicken eggs — and Goldenberg Peanut Chews. That also explains why the Goldenberg grandchildren are spending the summer right now at their beach houses in Ventnor while all I got is a lean-to in Maine.

JULY 15

The Road Not Taken

We drove to the town of Middlebury to eat at The Dog Team restaurant, which we visited on a family vacation years ago. As we walked from the car to the restaurant, we bumped into our old friend Steve. He was hitching west — alone. He and Al (and therefore Lance) split up and neither of them will be rejoining the Trail. That leaves only Steve Jackson ahead of us out of all those who left Baxter State Park before we did. And unless someone catches up, we will hike alone for the rest of the journey.

Steve and Al were two guys I thought would never split. We have all sorts of problems, but Steve and Al looked like they had it together. But what could I expect from two guys who stopped to smell the flowers — and then ate them.

After lunch, we visited the home of Robert Frost, the Poet Laureate of the Kennedy Administration. He used a small cabin in the Green Mountains to get away from distractions. Now, his woods holds a visitor center and dormitories to accommodate writers' workshops.

I read an interview with Leon Uris, one of my favorite

authors. He said, "So you want to be a writer. I'll put you into the business; I'll give you your first paper and pencil. After that, it is up to you. Write. Put the seat of your pants in a chair and write. There is no other way. So write."

He definitely never attended a writer's workshop.

I once bought my father a collection of Robert Frost's writings for his birthday. They had a print of one of his poems hanging on the wall of the main building:

> *TWO roads diverged in a yellow wood,* (Boy, don't I know it. How many times have I lost the Trail in a yellow wood? And in a green wood, and a grey wood, a black wood…)
>
> *And sorry I could not travel both.* (Not me. I just don't want to get lost in the woods.)
>
> *And be one traveler, long I stood*
>
> *And looked down one as far as I could.* (No need. Just follow the white blazes.)
>
> *To where it bent in the undergrowth;*
>
> *Then took the other, as just as fair,*
>
> *And having perhaps the better claim,*
>
> *Because it was grassy and wanted wear;* (It's probably not a road at all, unless it is one of those "lumber roads" in Maine.)
>
> *Though as for that the passing there*
>
> *had worn them really about the same,* (So they are the same. Just pick one and stop standing there.)
>
> *And both that morning equally lay*

in leaves no step had trodden black.

Oh, I kept the first for another day!

Yet knowing how way leads on to way,

I doubted if I should ever come back. (How often have I said I would revisit a lake or a beautiful setting? Whom am I kidding?)

I shall be telling this with a sigh;

somewhere ages and ages hence:

Two roads diverged in a wood, and I —

I took the one less traveled by,

And that has made all the difference.
(The problem I have with this poem is that every time I read it, the ink gets smeared.)

My only other visit to Vermont came seven years ago when my family camped near the town of Vergennes, on a bluff overlooking Boothbay Harbor on Lake Champlain. I was going into ninth grade and my interests were split between girls and baseball. Knowing this, my father offered to buy me one of that summer's two bestsellers for our vacation reading. The summer before, we all read *The Godfather* by Mario Puzo. This year, he bet my sister which book I would pick. The choices he gave me were *The Happy Hooker*, the colorful autobiography by Xaviera Hollander or *The Summer Game*, a book about the Brooklyn Dodgers by Roger Angel. I thought carefully about my response.

"I'll take *The Summer Game.*"

My father's jaw dropped and my sister let out, "I knew it!" Later I explained my reasoning to my sister. I chose the baseball book figuring Dad would buy the *Happy Hooker* anyway. So that summer I got to read both.

My sister received a great education observing — and egging on — my negotiations with my father. When I was ten, I was making twenty-five cents a week from my allowance, most of which I spent on baseball cards. But around then, I joined a stamp collecting club that proved to be a more expensive hobby; I felt keenly hampered by my lack of funds. Up until then, my collecting consisted of gluing stamp hinges on the backs of cancelled stamps I would purchase by the bagful, but the club exposed me to real collectors who slipped mint sets into sleek plastic sleeves. My meager income could no longer cut it. So I spoke with my big sister who assured me that if I discuss this with my father and explain my needs, he would grant me a raise. I thought I presented myself well and asked for eighty cents a week. He countered with thirty-five. Thus began my first negotiation with the Man. I dropped my demands to fifty cents but he wouldn't budge. Exasperated, I hit him with all I could muster: "If I can't have fifty, then I won't take anything at all!"

He replied, "Okay, I can live with that," and he walked out of the room.

I stood there dumfounded, trying to figure out what had just gone wrong when my sister slapped me on the back and said, "Good for you; stick to your principles." Then she too left the room, laughing.

JULY 17

Tamarack Shelter

What a joyous feeling to put it all together — the strength

of six weeks of walking and the freshness of starting anew. My boots now have new soles and fastidious waterproofing. My big toes are no longer covered with infected blisters. The swelling in my ankles disappeared as suddenly and as mysteriously as it appeared. Was it the antihistamine, the Dolomite, or the binding pressure of my boots? I have a new hip band for my pack so I will not have to bear as much of the weight on my shoulders anymore.

With the above maladies cured, walking should be fun again. We have seven days to hike one hundred miles to our next food drop, much of which is over level ground. This means short days with lots of energy and time for reading, writing, and enjoying the outdoors.

My parents walked with us from the campsite to the entrance to the Trail. My father hoped to walk for a few miles but my mother needed to turn back. This meant my father had to turn back after a few yards. I gave him a hug and he kissed me on my head. If I could have a second lifetime, I would want to do something like this with him.

I had the chance when I was younger, but I blew it. The troop went to Philmont, the national scout reservation in New Mexico. I was not keen on hiking in the hot desert, worrying about where I would find my next drink of water; I hate thirst over all deprivations. So, my dad, who was the scoutmaster, took ten other boys to New Mexico. I will never make up for that loss. It also questioned my courage. I did not fight in Vietnam. I did not go to Philmont. So here I am, like Harry Feversham in *The Four Feathers*, having to prove I am not a coward.

I can see the pride in my father's eyes over my great adventure; this time, I will not let him down. I was tempted to tell my partner to finish the Trail on his own, drive home with my parents, and get on with my life. But I can see that my Dad is following this hike as if he were doing it himself, so I did not even suggest a change. I will keep going for him.

Anyway, I had agreed to accompany Rand on this hike and "A promise made is a debt unpaid." I do not want to be a quitter and I do not want to go back on my word. Nevertheless, as Emerson once said, "A foolish consistency is the hobgoblin of little minds."

CHAPTER FIVE

Resurrection

JULY 18

Heat Wave

I am writing by the beautiful Little Rock Pond from which I emerged a few minutes ago.

I have made a clinical study of the causes of the recent swelling of my feet. While walking yesterday, I was bitten on the right thumb by a deer fly. My thumb swelled instantly. Although it did not hurt, it became difficult to bend. I bound into action swallowing an antihistamine pill. Within ten minutes, the swelling diminished. (While I write this, a chipmunk not more than six inches from my hand is licking the peanut butter off my knife.) Could a deer fly have caused the elephantiasis-like swelling in my ankles? My latest theory is that a deer fly bit me on some part of my body, then the toxins transferred to the already overworked tissues in my legs turning me into Big Foot. I now carry enough antihistamines to ward off the effects of these bug bites and the Dolomite to heal my minerally-impaired tissues.

Enough about bug bites. Now is the time for dreaming, for slipping into my thoughts about the past month on the Trail. All I have are dreams. I could not hold a conversation here even if I wanted to; the roar of my Svea stove would drown out my voice. Of course, I am all alone, so if I talked out loud, the squirrels would think I am a nut and carry me away.

I like to dream of dinner for two along the bank of a pond somewhere; two quiet voices drifting into space; a couple of lonely travelers meeting for the night, exchanging stories, then parting with the sun without any messy complications like having to trade the rest of my Logan Bread and peanut butter for some fudge. I am still waiting for Pam Nelson, the girl with whom I scheduled a dinner date when my southbound trek meets her northbound.

At times I wonder if I am strange, choosing to knock myself out climbing mountains. Some days are not too bad. What could beat walking alongside the cascading Eliza Brook, valiantly resisting its efforts to lure me in for a swim? The water sure looked refreshing as it bounced from rock to rock on its race to wherever.

There have been days when I have resisted the temptation to take off my pack and go for a swim, but there have been plenty when I gave in. I saw a newspaper headline about the tremendous heat wave gripping the country, causing riots and lootings in Manhattan. Meanwhile, here I am hiking through Vermont under tall trees, along cascading streams, and around cool, clear mountain lakes. I love Vermont's Green Mountains with its gentle slopes and green trail, but even here I have felt the effects of the summer's heat.

When I left Gifford State Park, I carried a pack into the Green Mountains filled with a week's supply of food, all sorts of munchies, and a new library of paperback books. In return, I gave my parents the binoculars, my down parka, and my wool pants. Still, I gained more weight than I shed and I have suffered from the excess. Carrying a heavy pack in muggy weather results in sweaty clothes. Walking in sweaty clothes leads to chafing, a painful condition that kills the joy of hiking. Yesterday, near the end of my third day in the Green Mountains, my enjoyment reached its all-time low. Climbing a mountain late in the afternoon, holding the bottom of my shorts to prevent any further rubbing between my legs, I knew I would not reach the lean-to before dark waddling like a duck. In the name of modesty I walked off the trail to coat my chafed thighs with a few drops of Dr. Bronner's Castile Peppermint soap; yet another of its thousands of uses. This soothed in a painful sort of way. Towel drying was impossible — too painful: my thighs hurt because of too much rubbing. So there I stood ten feet from the combination of the Long Trail and the AT with my shorts to my knees letting the late afternoon breeze waft through my legs.

Once seemingly healed, I set off along the Trail again, hoping to make up for lost time. But once again my damp shorts rubbed against my legs. There I was, a few miles from the lean-to but at a loss for answers. I knew the shorts had to go but my towel was too tiny to wrap around my waist. Of course, I would not dream of hiking in the nude — but then again, why not? After all, I had not seen another hiker for several hours and probably would not see another all night. But how could a guy who never mooned a passing car in his life, a guy so shy he goes into a closet just to change his mind — how could he hike four miles in his birthday suit? I took my shorts off and stuffed them in my pack.

So I walked to Little Rock Pond Shelter with nothing on but my hat hoping I would avoid other hikers. But just in case, I planned to stare at the other hiker's clothes while I shook my head in disgust, or say to the hiker, "You know what I like most about hiking the Trail? The total freedom."

JULY 19

Theories on Hitching

With all the miles I have walked so far it might seem strange that I have become an expert on riding in cars. But I have done a lot of hitch — in addition to the other kind of — hiking.

My first hitchhike came along Interstate 95 from the airport in Bangor to the Orono exit. This was thanks to a marine sergeant who saw our signs — *Mt. Katahdin, Please* and *AT Thruhikers* — and wanted to be the first to help us along our way. He sure was a big help, all right. He took us from the heavily traveled exit in Bangor to a ghost town five miles north. After two hours of fruitless thumbing in the mid-day sun, we walked to the next exit, Oldtown, in hope of better luck and maybe a Tastee-Freeze. The rules posted by the exit prohibited walking on the shoulder along the Interstate so we walked on the steep grade just below the shoulder. This twisted my boot so much it pinched my toes, causing the first of a long line of blisters. (It is true. You always remember your first.)

We finally got a ride from two guys who lived in a town two hundred miles north of Bangor. They said they picked us up because they felt sorry for us. They noticed us while driving in the southbound lane of I-95, heading to the hospital in Bangor. One of them, not the driver, had broken his leg. After the setting of the leg and the making of the cast, they saw we were still pathetically trying to thumb a ride. I told them we flew from Philadelphia to Bangor in less time than it took us to hitch the ten miles from Bangor to Oldtown.

Since then I have hitched into and out of a number of towns such as Stratton and Warren. I did not have to hitch into Manchester, however. Today was what I call an in-betweener, sort of a vacation day from the ardors of the Trail. We walked ten miles in less than four hours, so after meeting at the road that crossed the mountain range, we decided to eat lunch in town. While we washed up in a conveniently-placed creek, an old timer wandered over to chat with us. He let us know that he worked on the crew that originally blazed the Vermont section of the Trail. When we asked him about Manchester, he insisted on giving us a ride.

Sitting at Friendly's munching a hamburger and fries, I began to compose my theory on hitchhiking.

My theory begins with the assumption that backpackers represent a better class of people than mere hitchhikers. This holds doubly true near the Appalachian Trail, where the hitchhiking backpacker may be a man of destiny, the Knight Templar of backpackers — the Thruhiker. Unlike the rest of the crazies one might find hitchhiking, we use up all our craziness carrying eighty pound packs in hot, muggy weather.

Not everyone gives rides, not even to the most deserving of hitchhikers like me. I have stood many hours in the hot sun or the drenching rain trying to thumb a ride. Women; women with children; men with women and children; out-of-staters; and out-of-staters who are with women and children never give rides to hitchhikers. I do not know why this is so, but that has been my experience culled from numerous observations. Those who pick us up were men usually driving pickup trucks or vans. These men typically had facial hair and a wild look in their eyes.

I love the Green Mountains even though they did not have the alpine feel of the White Mountains of New Hampshire. In New Hampshire, while standing on top of the five thousand foot Mt. Lafayette, far above the tree line, I looked in awe at the magnificent Presidential Mountain Range spread across Grafton Notch. With so many parallel ridges and such deep notches, I felt like I was jumping waves. There were no waves in Vermont. Even the highest of the Green Mountain peaks are covered with trees. Even atop the fire tower on Mt. Glastonbury, I could not tell I was on a mountain. The valleys were filled with mist, robbing me of the contrast, so for all I could tell, I was looking over a flat, tree-filled forest.

The actual hiking, though, has been fun. The long gentle stretches of ambling have left me with plenty of energy at the end of each day. The weather has been too hot to be called perfect, but this has made the already tempting lakes and streams all the more so. That was why I will be happy to return to the Trail later today even though Manchester was a charming town. I actually prefer the beauty of the Trail to the sidewalks of a town. No longer are we so removed from civilization that the simple joys of having cold beer appear only in my fantasies. The Long Trail is frequently intersected by roads that lead downhill to towns. Although I no longer invade a town like a hungry bear, I still enjoy sampling good foods, browsing through a book store — Manchester has two — or sitting next to a cold beer. Manchester has numerous bakeries, cheese shops, and grocery stores. Even though there must be a thousand things I would love to buy, I pass, because I am determined to rid myself of my last big pain, an overstuffed pack. Despite leaving my binoculars and several other nonessentials with my folks at Gifford Woods, my pack weighs more now than ever, even more than the colossal sixty-one pounds I carried into the White Mountains out of Gorham. Since leaving Gifford, I have wrapped an Ace bandage around my knee for support.

I tried to lighten my load after Gifford by eating the entire one pound bag of peanut M&Ms in one sitting. I did not intend to eat them all, but once I opened the bag, I needed to get rid of those multicolor ovals that were egging me on to eat just one more. The one pound transfer from my pack to my stomach did not immediately reduce the burden on my legs.

I made an adjustment to my brand new nylon pocket. I put too much faith in Velcro. The weight of the guidebook along with the vibrations of walking gradually loosened the pocket from the strap until it tumbled to the ground. At least this took place in front of me and so I could catch the pocket, unlike, say, my moccasins, my socks, my tee-shirt (I could go on) which have fallen off the back of my pack. I fixed the pocket easily enough by winding a thin cord under the top flap then tied the cord to the top of the pack frame.

On the ride into Manchester, I observed the farms that filled the valley. My father spent the summer of 1943 in Manchester working on the farm owned by the great granddaughter of Abraham Lincoln. He was fifteen. Before then he travelled no farther from Philadelphia than Atlantic City, sixty miles east. That summer he pitched hay, picked crops, cut wood, and did whatever else needed to get done. At fifteen, he would rather have joined the Marines but instead settled for taking the place of other young men, a few years older, who shipped overseas to fight the evil that infected the nations of the world.

Every night, Miss Lincoln gave dad some money and he would walk into town to eat dinner. Manchester at that time was a town center not just for farmers, but for artists, authors and, as my dad would learn, his heroes.

A year earlier, my father earned money — and won a hatchet in a contest — from selling and delivering subscriptions to *The Saturday Evening Post*. In the age before television, everyone awaited the weekly *Evening Post* to gaze upon the cover, frequently illustrated by Norman Rockwell, as big a media star as there was back then. His covers for the *Saturday Evening Post* captured emotions that struck deep in the hearts of Americans. He told our story in pictures, one week at a time.

Over my bed at home hung a poster showing a Pirates-Dodgers game, with Pittsburgh holding the slimmest of leads. The two managers crowded around the chief umpire who looked skyward, determining whether the first drops of rain would lead to more, forcing him to call the game and award Pittsburgh the victory. The Pirates manager, scowling, huddled miserably under the impending downpour. Meanwhile, the Dodger manager, with a carefree smile, pointed to the one ray of sunlight poking through the clouds. That poster was a reprint of a *Saturday Evening Post* cover by Norman Rockwell. Each day that picture reminded me that every problem depends on one's perspective: "Where you stand depends upon where you sit."

The bookstore we visited in Manchester had a special display table holding a large portfolio book of Rockwell paintings. He drew America, capturing the way we laughed, the way we relaxed, the way we worked, and the way we worried. He provided the illustrated version of our Constitution, our Bill of Rights, and the Four Freedoms we hold dear in this country. We have Rockwell's depiction of one of those Freedoms, the Freedom of Religion, hanging in the study of our home. If America is the home of the brave and the land of the free, Rockwell was the person who put those thoughts to the colored page. Imagine then, that a fifteen year old boy. who just the year before delivered the *Saturday Evening Post* from his bike, ate his meal every night a few feet away from where Norman Rockwell came to drink coffee and chat with his friends in Manchester, Vermont.

The only possessions my father kept from his teen years was a baseball Ted Williams hit into the stands at Shibe

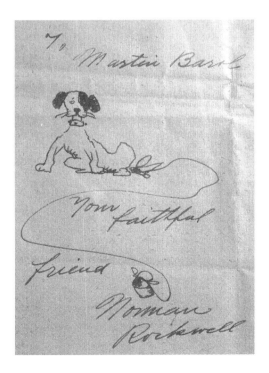

Park, my grandfather's baseball glove and bat, and a framed sheet of stationery with a handwritten sketch of a dog and a note that reads, "To Martin Barol, from your faithful friend, Norman Rockwell."

When we finally pulled ourselves away from this wonderful New England town, we walked to the edge of town along the road that would take us up to where we left the Trail.

Actually, hitching can be fun. It offers all the suspense of fishing with none of the scales to clean. It provides a great way to meet people, pick up local news, and find a good place to eat. But my main concern on Route 11 out of Manchester was to convince people that I looked honest. Ever try to look honest? Because we hid our packs in the woods, we were just another pair of bums thumbing by the side of the road, sporting unkempt hair and scrawny beards.

Finally a car stopped. "Odd," I thought as I ran to where it stopped, "it has a Texas license plate, an out-of-stater." Not only that, I saw as I got closer, the driver was a woman. Then, as I was about to open the door, I saw a little girl strapped into the back seat. This was an outrage. I was all set to turn the ride down when Rand jumped into the front seat. What happened to principles? Like buses, there will always be another ride, but good theories are hard to come by.

JULY 21

Williamstown

I have no idea how far I walked today due to the many changes in the Trail. These ever changing routes, along with the flies, are the only negatives about Vermont, otherwise it is the vacation spot of the AT. The paths are smooth and the climbs gradual with plenty of switchbacks. Trees shade the Trail, ponds and streams abound, and there have been enough people to keep loneliness at bay. The only sore spot has been that the person I should be sharing this joy with has become increasingly sullen and unfriendly. I decided to never bring up or even think about the fudge or the Old Lumber Camp; nevertheless, we are walking separate trips, only coming together at each day's destination. We live in separate worlds, the one cloud on an otherwise sunny day.

The Trail goes by Williams College, a pretty campus of grey stone buildings and well-manicured lawns. We will wait until dark, then roll our sleeping bags out.

I feel energized when I visit a college campus, like I have all the hope in the world. I want to use that potential. I do not want to look back on my life and say "I could've been some-body." I no longer think life is about doing what you love. The meaning of life is doing what you, and you alone, deem important. I need to look no further for an example than my father. He lives his calling all day long.

What do I know about him? What makes him tick?

He was two years old when the country plunged into the Great Depression followed by the second all-out war of the century. His heroes were Lou Gehrig, the Pride of the Yankees; FDR; Churchill; Norman Rockwell; and, later, Martin Luther King.

When it came to local sports heroes in Philadelphia, his father, Dave Barol, played baseball professionally before World War I, then played for the Navy during the war. My dad was a good ballplayer but not great like his father. (The baseball gene continued to dissipate by the time it reached me.) He captained the Overbrook High School baseball team, modeling himself at first base after his hero Lou Gehrig, but baseball shaped him in other ways.

As a young boy, he listened to his father talk about traveling around the country playing against the many leagues that existed during the 1910s and 1920s. My grandfather would tell how they used to treat a player bleeding from a spike wound in those days by pulling away the torn, bloodied pants leg then spitting tobacco juice into it. (Although Lister had already discovered germs, the news was slow to reach the International League.)

He told my father stories about games played against the Negro Leagues, a separate but supposedly equal world. Across the diamond from my grandfather sat people whose ancestors came to this country unwillingly and then worked without regard for their aspirations or talents, without either compensation or access to capital. Decades after the end of formalized slavery, they were still denied the opportunity to employ their skills and passions, even in the game of baseball. This struck a chord deep within my dad, because as a "pretty good country ballplayer" himself, he competed based on ability, not on race or religion. Baseball mattered to him, but a game that separated people by race would not become his life's passion. What burned inside of him was the desire to make our country great, both in war and in peace, not just for White people, not just for Jews, or Democrats — but for all Americans.

My father did not play baseball during his senior year, but instead served his school and his community. His fellow students elected him President of Overbrook High School for 1944-45, a time when many professional ball players left the game to serve their country. After graduation, he joined the Navy.

When he made sure the world was safe, the Navy helped him go to college and then to law school before needing him again in Korea. His second tour began before he could sit for the bar exam, so instead of serving as a lawyer in the Judge Advocate General Service, he went to Officer Candidate School in Newport to serve as a naval officer. That shaped his life, because he used his law degree more as training to run organizations than as a litigator; there always was a sense of the officer about him.

When my dad began practicing law, he defended poor people, represented social agencies, and took the causes that other lawyers could no longer afford to pursue in the "Real World." One such acquaintance from law school passed him in a court room and asked, "Still tilting at windmills, Marty?"

There was not a lot of money to be made saving the world, but we never went hungry and we have more books at home than we could possibly read. I never once heard him covet someone else's wealth. In fact, he was happy for other people's successes because he was confident in his own skin; he was his own man; he followed his own dream; and that is what mattered most to him.

JULY 24

Cheshire Village

Cheshire is not a big spot on the AAA map of places to visit in Massachusetts, but it was here that the Cheshire cheese was made, the half-ton cheese the town presented to Thomas Jefferson at the White House. They even have a scale replica of the cheese press used to make the cheese. All that said, cheese played only a small part in my being in Cheshire. I arrived here to eat breakfast at Friendly's after walking seven miles from the top of Mount Greylock, where we spent last night.

At an elevation of 3,490 feet, Greylock is the tallest mountain in Massachusetts. After all the hiking I have done, 3,400 feet is more of an inconvenience than a climb but Greylock refused to be taken lightly. The sides were steep, rising more than 2,000 feet above the surrounding valley. On top sits the Memorial Beacon with its large glass globe that lights up after dark. The lodge on top was probably the in-thing in the early years of the twentieth century. A road winds its way to the top, which the Trail crosses. The views from Greylock are beautiful and from the top I could see in all directions. But I did not race up Greylock for the views.

Picture a steak sizzling on an open fire, a loaf of bread, a jug of wine, a beautiful girl in a flowery dress — a painting by Monet? This really happened last night. A wonderful young woman brought gentility to the AT. What a far cry from eating macaroni in a Maine swamp.

Didi Osgood, whose father teaches at nearby Mt. Holyoke College, lived in the same dorm we did, although a year later. She met us on top of Greylock with our food cache and the perfect dinner. We agreed to meet at three in the afternoon, an easy enough time to climb the mountain, considering we camped only six miles to the north, but nevertheless I made it difficult considering I did not leave Friendly's until noon.

Chugging up Greylock took a lot of determination. The people I passed along the way were amused that I was running late for a dinner date. Some, who already spoke with my partner, guessed the reason for my haste and cheered me on to my goal. I kept playing the Mad Hatter song in my head, "I'm late, I'm late. For a very important date . . ." While approaching the summit, I could see the beacon tower beckoning. As I passed it, I threw up my hands in exultation, like a sprinter breaking a tape. Climbing Greylock in under three hours was no easy task. I walked into Baskin Lodge, but saw neither Didi nor my partner, so I went to the men's room to wash up and change into a dry tee shirt. Rand was eating a cheeseburger at the snack counter when I came out, so I joined him seeking to quench my vicious thirst. I asked the guy behind the bar, how big a slice of watermelon I could buy for twenty-five cents.

"Are you a Thruhiker?" he asked.

I nodded.

"Then how big do you want?"

I do not know if it was the watermelon or the service, but that sure tasted good. Just as I was slurping down my last section of melon, Didi walked in. A welcome from a bubbling person like her is as refreshing as chilled watermelon after a hard climb. Didi was full of questions and added lots besides. "Nancy (her equally vivacious and beautiful girlfriend) could not come because she had a dentist appointment and her aunt died and Jeff-somebody called to say he won't be able to meet you but will mail your food instead."

My plan was to meet Jeff in Pawling, New York, on Saturday night. If he already mailed the food there, we would be out of luck, because the earliest we could get there would be after the post office closes and we would then have to wait until it reopens Monday. I tried to reach him right away, but there was no answer.

Didi found a grassy knoll that was semi-private enough to commence our picnic. She brought a bottle of wine, a loaf of bread, steak, and peaches. All this, along with the grapes and cheese I brought comprised our splendid bill of fare and the start to a wonderful evening that came to an end way too soon. Both Rand and I could have spent the night just looking at her (once we consumed every crumb of bread, kernel of corn, drop of wine). Not only was she lovely to look at, but she made us food: ah, now that is a perfect catch. Didi was at the same time sophisticated and innocent, like a Grace Kelly character. Rand and I were both exhausted from our mad sprint up the mountain, then so satiated by the wonderful meal, that our conversation slowed and we both just gazed at her.

As the sun began to set, she left us so as not to take the steep, twisting road in the dark. As the sun went down, taking Didi with it, so did our spirits. Her absence left us with each other. We rolled our sleeping bags out on the same grassy knoll and went to sleep in silence.

JULY 26

Mystery Woman

I am leaning against my pack, overlooking Finnerty Pond on one of the most gorgeous days to follow a dreary one of rain. Finnerty is a clear mountain pond, surrounded by trees, as unspoiled today as when man first found it. The air is too cool for a swim, but I am enjoying this spot with my eyes alone.

There are many mysteries along the Appalachian Trail but the one that I wanted to solve the most was the one about the Mystery Woman. I heard about her from the Northbounders and read in the trail registers that if you can get to the October Mountain Lean-to at the right time, a woman will drive there and take Thruhikers to her home for a night's rest, a full meal, and a hot shower. They were all strangers to her, but her kindness was legendary. I was determined that no matter how tired I was on that day, I would keep going to reach the October Mountain Lean-to by day's end.

Such are plans, aren't they? When I reached the town of Dalton, a small town near Pittsfield, a larger town, I was still eleven miles north of the lean-to. It was already past four in the afternoon. I caught up to my partner, or rather he waited for me so we could confer. If we continued to walk fast, we would still not reach the lean-to until long dark, after she would have already gathered her night's lodgers. On the other hand, stopping here would mean we would pass the lean-to in the middle of the next day. To add to our deliberations, I had not reached Jeff about making new plans for our food drop. So instead of continuing on the Trail, we turned right and walked along a road looking for a public phone. Up ahead, I saw a woman get into her station wagon. "Excuse me," I called to her, "Can you direct me toward the closest pay phone?"

"Are you a Thruhiker?" she asked.

"Well, yes."

"Then you have a choice. You can either walk down the

road a mile and a half to the shopping center or you can use the one in my kitchen."

Mrs. Soules showed me the phone and then left to pick up her son from day camp. Strange, I thought, I am nowhere near the lean-to; could she be the Mystery Woman? I finally reached my friend Jeff and asked him to mail the box and any letters to the post office in Kent, Connecticut, Care of General Delivery: Appalachian Trail Hiker. I figured we would get there on a weekday.

This college buddy, who so enthusiastically volunteered his services, made plans to take a girl down the shore. Technically, he would not say he was "going down the shore" as he is not from Philadelphia. Jeff, a New Yorker, would definitely say he is "going to the beach." It is a peculiarity of Philadelphians to limit the word "beach" to the sandy area running along the ocean waves but to call the connection of communities along the New Jersey coast, including the boardwalks, the taffy shops, the piers, and guest houses — "the Shore." And when we travel to a lower elevation, no matter if it is lower by inches, we Philadelphians say we are heading "down" and we do not bother with the superfluous word "to." So, when we head into center city, we say we are "going down Philly." When we head for a week of seaside relaxation and enjoyment, we say we are "going down the shore."

Vacationing is like a genetic ailment. For some families, everyone vacations at the same place for decades. For other families, like mine, vacationing skips generations. When my parents were kids, their families would go down the shore every summer. And yet, I can count on one hand the number of days I have spent down the shore. It seemed that my dad would rather take us to the moon than take us back down the shore. I have spent summers in Maine, Vermont, Tennessee, Virginia — but not down the Jersey shore, sixty miles from my home.

When Mrs. Soules returned a few minutes later, she offered us the use of her backyard for the night. No Mystery Woman here. We considered pressing on to the lean-to; not that I knew the Mystery Woman would come; maybe she went down the shore as well. Oh well, not all mysteries get solved.

Mrs. Soules was an attractive woman so full of grace and kindness she made my heart ache. She was married to the Reverend Mr. Soules, a Congregationalist minister. When he got home he came out to meet us. He was very kind and sat down on the lounge chair to talk about our journey. He seemed compelled to lead the discussion toward a certain direction. Finally, he asked me if I used a guide to follow my path. I showed him the Appalachian Trail Guide to Massachusetts and Connecticut, complete with maps.

"I also follow a guide," he said, taking his bible out of his jacket. He then left me with a couple pamphlets to read, all in good Congregationalist fun.

Dinner was cooking on our one-burner Svea stove when the Reverend Mr. and Mrs. Soules came out with a plate of corn muffins. I do not know what they expected, but their jaws dropped when they saw me stirring our casserole of chicken, tomatoes, onion, zucchini, and bulgur wheat, while my partner put the finishing touches on a chocolate cream pie. Nevertheless, the muffins were a welcome addition.

Although it looked like rain, we did not pitch the tent in the back yard. If the good Reverend Mr. Soules wanted divots, I am sure he would have taken up golf. Unfortunately, sometime after dark but before light, I felt the first drop of rain. Now unlike us Southbounders, rain drops travel in large groups. I pulled my ground cover over my sleeping bag and crawled onto a chaise lounge. This was one way to beat having to bring a tent along, but strapping a chaise lounge to my pack would create problems of its own. Besides, it probably would have fallen off my pack in Maine. (Did that state go on forever — or what?)

Since it rained all morning, and the next section of the Trail was a renowned swamp, we walked the mile and a half to the Coltesville Mall. There we went to a Friendly's Restaurant (our third in a week) for breakfast and later browsed through a bookstore. My partner had received a check from his grandmother at the last post office. Rand was hiking in search of solitude, and so it was natural — to him — to leave all trappings of civilization behind. Unfortunately, the bank required two such "trappings" to cash his check.

Luckily I carried both my driver's license and a couple of credit cards, so I told him to endorse the check to me. I then handed the young lady my requisite two forms of identification, and collected the cash, which I then handed to him. Neither of us argued the point with her but just took the money and slowly walked away.

It was a dark day and it rained hard into the afternoon. My father used to say days like this were "good for the crops." We never grew crops in our backyard in Philadelphia so I never held the same affection for a soaking rain that left us cold and shivering on our walk home from school. But that was then; now we had a Trail to hike. After walking back from the mall, we collected our packs from the house of Soules, leaving the town of Dalton for good.

We had spent the morning sitting at Friendly's and

browsing a bookshop together. I helped him out at the bank and I know without question he would have done the same for me. Yet, as soon as we started hiking on the Trail, he walked off without so much as a wave until he was out of sight.

Nevertheless, as I write about this now, I have either gone past caring or decided holding on to these grudges sours a beautiful view and poisons whatever good thoughts I can keep in my head. Maybe I am not equipped to handle both good and bad thoughts in my brain at the same time. As of now, I will never dwell on fudge or lumber camps again.

I have allowed this relationship to color my view of the world around me for days on end. Not anymore; I have chosen not to dwell on my relationship with my partner anymore. I do not care if we hike together or even if he shows up tonight. If we split, like Steve and Al did, I am sure we could easily figure out what to do. We passed enough Northbounders to know that it is not only possible but preferable to hike alone on the Trail. I do not know how I can break this partnership up since it was he who asked me to join. I do not want anyone to think I am a quitter or a backstabber.

The Trail south of Dalton was indeed swampy, the most Maine-like since Maine. To top off the mud and rain, I brushed past so many overhanging bushes that even during the lulls in the storm, I was still getting soaked. Usually I do not mind hiking in the rain; if I were not used to it after Maine I would never be. But this rain was cold and its drops were big and every step meant pulling my feet from the muck with a sucking sound. If ever I could have used the Mystery Woman, it was then. The rain had fallen on me since the middle of the night and I was feeling chilled and very tired.

I needed to press on to the lean-to. The thought crossed my mind that suppose she went on a vacation? Or worse, what if she stopped by the lean-to before I got there? I pushed myself to walk faster.

Forests are different during the rain. They have a dull silence: the crickets stop chirping and the birds sit still. The only noise comes from the sounds of the drops and they are so rhythmic they blend into the background. Without the sun, the colors lose their glow; everything becomes subdued. The nylon blinders of my overhanging poncho fix my gaze straight ahead. Even then I look down not wanting the rain to pour into my eyes.

With my gaze down, I smacked into a tall bush drooping over the path. I reached to push the bush to the side when I realized it was no ordinary bush. It was a twelve foot high blueberry bush covered with the plumpest, juiciest blueberries I have ever seen let alone brushed up against. I stuffed my mouth with rain-chilled berries bursting with blueberry flavor. Then I filled my quart sized plastic water jug as well.

When the Trail crossed the hard paved Washington Mountain Road, I took the advice of several Northbounders who said to stay on the road to avoid the swampy sections. The rain stopped and the sun was trying to poke through the clouds. As I walked past houses deeply set from the road, one dog after another barked at my passing. A black and white dog with long ears came down a driveway to get a closer bark at me. I barked back and obviously said the right thing because she tilted her head and wagged her short tail. I went down on one knee and she came up to me, sniffed my outstretched hand, and then leaned against me as I scratched behind her ears saying, "You don't want to hurt nobody; you don't even want to hurt nobody."

She was an English springer spaniel, perhaps the most beautiful of all the breeds, and she was an excellent example, with a wide blaze of white fur between her eyes and down her nose. Her white chest hair, having been recently brushed, flowed like the ruffles. When I stopped scratching, she put her paw on my knee and looked at me with sad eyes, so I kept at it for a while longer. She gave my face a lick and I gave her a hug and said goodbye to her forever.

Because of the rain, I kept my watch in a plastic bag, so I had no idea what time it was. I was tired, muddy, and so wet

I was feeling chilled. I was in need of more comfort than I was going to find in some smelly old lean-to. "Please Mystery Woman; don't fail me."

With the barking from every house, I would not be sneaking up on anybody along this road. I passed a house with a porch running around its second story, like an alpine lodge. A woman called out to me.

"Are you Carl?"

I looked around. "You talking to me? No. I'm not Carl." I kept walking but this time a little old man ran down the steps yelling for me to wait.

"Where'd you hike from?" He looked like Popeye the Sailor Man from childhood cartoons.

"From Dalton. I left there at one."

"You telling me you hiked all of eleven miles and you look like this? You must have been hiking before Dalton."

Through my cold and fatigue I smiled. "Before Dalton? . . . Let's see now . . . I believe the Indians called it — 'Katahdin.'"

The little man's face lit up. "I knew it, Midge," he called to the woman on the porch. "He's the first Southbounder of the year."

I felt like a duck.

He told me to wait while he fetched his camera. Despite my protests that Steve Jackson was the first, Charles Fisher of Florham Park, New Jersey, took my picture.

"Well, you're the first Southbounder I've seen, so that makes you official. Now take off your pack and stick it on the porch. I want you to meet a wonderful lady."

I took a long hot shower while Midge and Charley drove to the lean-to for my partner and Carl, a tall Northbounder from Tennessee. Midge knew when a Thruhiker was due from the south. Her girlfriend in Tyringham, thirteen miles south, kept a trail register in her general store. Of course, no self-respecting Thruhiker would pass up a general store, so they had themselves a fool-proof early warning system.

Midge put our clothes through the washer and drier, and then made us a hearty dinner. We sat around the table talking for hours. (Although my partner, not feeling well after a night and day in the rain, stared glassy-eyed, not saying a word.)

At sixty-four, Charley was realizing his lifelong dream of becoming a Thruhiker. For years he hiked the Trail in bits and pieces, but could never satisfy his dream. So finally his wife told him to go ahead already, hoping he would finally get the AT bug out of his system. He was among the first to leave Georgia this year but since he hiked no more than ten miles a day, just about every Northbounder we met had passed him. I told him several Northbounders had warned me to look out for him. He told me to look out for the only two hikers he passed.

"There are two nurses known on the Trail as the "Snail Sisters," he told us. "They walked off their jobs one day and haven't stopped walking since."

"I look forward to meeting them more than I do reaching Georgia," I said, my eyes drifting in dreamy anticipation. I asked him if he happened to exchange places with a young woman named Pam, but he said no.

The next morning I coaxed Midge into using my blueberries to cook pancakes. She pulled out a quart of her brother's homemade maple syrup, rounding out a classic New England breakfast.

Back on the Trail heading south again, already well behind

my partner, I passed the October Mountain Lean-to: it was small, dark, and damp. The ground around it was the consistency of oatmeal and there was no drinking water nearby. If I reached that lean-to after a day of hiking, I would have kept going.

According to Charley, Midge lost her husband, and not having anyone to care for, became increasingly depressed. Her doctor and family pleaded with her to get involved in living again, but she could not bring herself to volunteer anywhere. Then one day, as she stared out her window, she saw a solitary hiker limping past. Even from where she sat, she could see that he looked even more discouraged than she, that after all the miles he must have hiked, he would probably quit because he hurt his leg. She caught up to him and coaxed him to her home. After a few warm meals and the chance to mend his strained muscles, he was on the road again, full of hope and vigor. And so was she.

JULY 30

The Approaching Storm

Connecticut abounds with rolling hills, beautiful scenes, and picturesque towns. On each of the past two days, I walked through ravines: Sage's on the Connecticut-Massachusetts border, and Dean's, in the Housatonic State Forest. Both ravines were spectacular — as wild as anything in Maine. Rushing creeks cascade through steep valleys and fall into pools, churning white against the rocks. Tall trees shade the Trail, keeping the summer heat at bay. That such physical beauty exists in Connecticut took me by surprise, but to walk through it, to experience it, has beckoned me to come back.

My only other experience with Connecticut was stopping in New Haven. I was on my way with my friend Rob Perry to go skiing over winter break when we paid Judy Garber a surprise visit. Judy had been a resident advisor in our dorm my first year. She just started medical school at Yale and was delighted for the interruption. She told us how much she missed the University of Virginia. "Snow," she said, "should fall on grass and trees, not roof tops and parking garages." That did not leave me with a good impression of the Nutmeg State.

And yet over these past few days I have walked through incredible natural beauty. The Housatonic Valley once served as the summer getaway for some of the country's most creative people. Many of the writers, singers, and artists who struggled with their crafts in Greenwich Village garrets, bought summer homes in this mist veiled valley once they achieved success. When I shopped at the Shagroy Supermarket in Salisbury, I marveled at the selection of fruits, meats, and gourmet foods usually sold only in specialty shops. Here, the everyday supermarket was a specialty shop. Slabs of smoked salmon, mangoes, and pâtés lined the shelves as the very wealthy, the very sophisticated — and I — made our selections.

I knew I entered a special community when after crossing the state line I mentioned to a bird watcher that I entered "my fifth state."

"Your fifth state of consciousness?" he asked.

People were not making snappy connections like that in Maine. Instead I got, "No milk here."

After sixty days on the Trail I have become aware of nature's orchestration. Take a thunderstorm, for instance.

The pink sky; the humid air; the fevered hum of the mosquitoes: these represent the prelude to the first drops of rain. The first drops fall one by one, then with greater intensity, thicker drops, colder drops. Lightning flashes and thunder rolls followed by the pelting steadiness of the downpour with its crescendos and lulls. And just when it seems that the storm will go on forever, shadows appear on the ground. The clouds take form once more allowing the sun to shine through. Melody replaces rhythm, as birds sing from their perches to the gurgling sounds of freshly swelled brooks and springs. And I hike on once more.

I am sitting out a late July storm in the Red Mountain Lean-to. But this will not be the only storm I will endure from this sheltered perch. I stopped at the lean-to after walking five miles — wet from the rain — but feeling fine otherwise. Here I wait for my partner to arrive. Like a thunderstorm, my relationship with him has gone through all the same stages. As I wait, I know we are well past the first drops.

I awoke at a quarter-to-five after a miserable night's sleep. The sky was pink, the air humid, and the mosquitoes buzzing around my ears were feasting on my hands and face, despite my mosquito netting. Those mosquitoes enjoyed a big laugh at my expense biting me through the netting that lay flat against my face. I tried to prop it up with my hat, but I could not breathe with my hat over my nose. Finally, I said "Nuts!" and pitched the tent. Five minutes later my partner joined me just before the sky opened with a terrific downpour.

The tent we carry is a clever collection of ideas. It has mosquito netting in the front, back and sides, all sheltered by a rainproof tarp. This means that the condensation from our breath and sweat passes through the tent's walls but the tarp keeps the rain out. Some older models attempted to both breathe and repel rain with one layer. The problem with that vintage was that any contact with the material let the rainwater seep through the canvass. There were also tents that were totally waterproof but did not "breathe." These do not let water in but they also do not let water out, leaving clothes and sleeping bags damp from the moisture of our bodies.

Rand was still asleep when I awoke a second time, so I pulled my pack out of the tent, got dressed outside, and then stuffed my sleeping bag into its sack — again outside the tent. I scurried about packing up, so that I could be on the Trail before the approaching storm hit.

Stuffing a sleeping bag into a sack makes some noise — not a whole lot — but some. I was not singing or anything like that. In fact, several flocks of squawking geese passed overhead in search of drier ponds, drowning out whatever rustling sounds I was making. Just as a particularly noisy flock passed by, my partner stuck his head out of the tent and said, "You are the most inconsiderate person I have ever met. First you wake me in the middle of the night pitching the tent, then you wake me early in the morning packing your bag."

"I am sorry to wake you but I pitched the tent because the mosquitoes kept biting me."

"They weren't bothering me — until you woke me."

Perhaps he just doesn't like mornings? I left as soon as the tent was rolled away telling him I would have breakfast ready at the next lean-to. I took off, whistling "Hey Baby," a popular song that played at every party at school.

I must admit I was proud of the way I handled the scene at the campsite. Maybe it was the Vitamin B supplements.

Rather than argue or sulk or attack the tent with a knife, I apologized, showed no resentment, and moved on. I was not going to mention the lumber camp or fudge.

My partner has been in a particularly foul mood these past few days. Although we have not been close at any time during the hike, he has become particularly sullen since leaving Greylock. I wish I could have spent that evening alone with Didi, perhaps he felt the same. Neither one of us wished to play wingman to the other. Didi was my friend from school and I arranged the meeting. It is not that she would have done anything untoward and certainly Didi was so effervescent she made the dinner delightful for both of us, but when you are as thirsty as we are, you want every drop for yourself.

I am writing with breakfast ready on the Svea stove: granola with milk powder — just add water, heat, and serve. I am enjoying some hot tea as I sit out the cold rain, although it is annoying to wait this long. I have waited here, about five miles from where we camped, for almost two hours, reading, writing, and sipping tea. And waiting. This is just not right.

Each day since entering Massachusetts our normally strained relationship has become increasingly rancorous. He rarely speaks to me in sentences, answering instead in a system of grunts and snorts, which I am actually beginning to understand. I think "huh" means "Do whatever the hell you want." A wide eyed look with a low rumble means, "Go fuck yourself." This proves once again that the best way to learn a language is to immerse oneself with the native speakers.

The real tragedy to all of this has been that we have missed so much of the Trail's beauty because of our smoldering ill will toward each other. We turned so many good days into bad, missing so much joy because of resentment. Each time we missed enjoying a scenic overlook or a hemlock studded ravine, because we were smothered by this personal conflict, caused us to resent the other even more.

The one thing I will not bring up — or even think about — is fudge or the lumber camp. That is actually two things.

I know I am not perfect but I really try to start each day fresh, with a song in my heart, a whistle on my lips, and a smile on my face. But I am at a loss as to how to resurrect our lost friendship.

JULY 30

The Storm Has Passed

Well, that's that.

Rand arrived at the lean-to two hours after me and now he has left. When he arrived, he was red faced and obviously worked up. Before I could say anything he told me to shut up and listen.

"There comes a time when two people can better help themselves..." "Fine," I said, "It'd be easy to split."

"Don't take away my satisfaction of suggesting it first. I've prepared a list of the things you have done."

He read his list of reasons why I was the ogre. I listened but excuse me for not taking notes. When a person writes a list, he has already decided what action he will take. The list serves more as a boost to his nerve than an outline for a discussion.

I had no idea he was so ticked at me for forcing him to spend the night at the Mystery Woman's house, whereas he was perfectly happy to stay in the lean-to. Right. To me, the Mystery Woman was the reason I crossed into Massachusetts; to him, it was a night feeling miserable and then having to hike over the same ground he had hiked the day before.

Much of the list consisted of things he would have felt about anyone with whom he would have hiked. The entire journey thus far felt like a prison to him, like he was shackled to me. He complained I controlled everything, made all the decisions, and acted like his scoutmaster.

How could we have avoided this? If he did not want to walk within earshot and we presumably are partners, then we needed to pick a place to meet each night. Neither of us brought walkie-talkies and my skills at mental telepathy lapsed some time ago. Yes, I planned the menus and arranged the food pickups, which meant we needed to get to certain places by certain times. I did not originate this concept; this is what people do when they hike the Appalachian Trail unless you are Steve Jackson and you hike seventy miles a day or the Doyle fellow, with your dad driving ahead in a Winnebago.

I guess when he asked me to join him, he lacked the confidence to go it alone or needed someone else to get the permission to live his dream. But once on the Trail, he realized — and I would certainly agree — there was no one more capable of hiking on his own, with the exception of Steve Jackson. Rand does not need for someone to chat with while he walks and certainly does not need to stare over a map to decide how far to hike each day. He could probably do this without the white blazes.

Although he was leading this discussion, he was heading in the direction I wanted to go. Too bad we saved our deepest discussion to last. When he finished his long list of griev-ances, we agreed to meet in Kent, some twenty-five miles south, to pick up the food Jeff mailed to the post office. We will divide it along with the shared equipment.

He left first this time as neither one of us wants to hitch together. I felt lonely hiking with someone; it will be interest-ing to see whether I will feel less lonely hiking alone.

JULY 31

Kent Congregationalist Church

I'm Free. I'm Free.
And Freedom tastes like Reality. - The Who

I am finally free from sour looks and muffled remarks. Free from negativity and condescension. I will now choose the company I wish to keep or stay alone if I like without the worry of having to meet someone at a given place or time. I can stop for the things I like, camp where I like, eat when and what I like. All restrictions of hiking with another are hereby dissolved. I am free.

Last night Rand reached Kent first and went to the post office to pick up our box of food, which he divided into two piles, and, always the gentleman, allowed me to pick which pile I wanted. We agreed that he would keep his tent and I would keep my stove and basically leave the rest of the equipment with whomever carried it. We then went out to eat dinner. We enjoyed our best conversation of the trip. He actually laughed at my story of going nose-to-nose with the moose. It was as if we renewed our lost friendship. Dinner sounded like singing birds and gurgling streams.

It was not a random event that sat us together on that

plane to Maine. He was one of the first people I met in college, someone I played tennis with, volleyball, Frisbee, and bridge. He is one of the most intelligent people I ever met; he truly is a rocket scientist. We lived next door to each other first year and in the same house for our second year. We would fight for each other, and yet, on the first day, he changed the dynamic when he said, "I hope you don't plan on stopping every time I do." We never were the Two Musketeers after that. In the absence of any other Southbounders surviving Maine, and the rarity of sharing the night with a Northbounder, this detachment made the hike a lonely experience. Spending all this time alone was something he looked forward to whereas I would not have chosen it in a million years.

To compound it all, there was the conflict over private property. Without thinking, I guess I decided the wellbeing of the community overrode the individual right to property, or, to put it simply, when I dared suggest he share his fudge with me. Yeah, he brought that up.

Bound together, we were bound for conflict. But was that our personalities at work or was every hiking partnership so doomed? Somehow there must be a way for partners to determine their hiking styles, their eating tastes, and how they will make decisions before actually setting forth into the woods. I must have missed that chapter in Colin Fletcher's book. I was certainly not smart enough to anticipate and talk this through before beginning our partnership.

For a long time, I thought the reason for our conflict was that we were starving, but it has been weeks since that was the case and our relationship continued to deteriorate. Although neither of us are the type to discuss our feelings, at least not with another guy, had we done so, maybe we would have learned how to survive together.

Had he joined me for that dry run, it would have given us a taste of our life together. We would have either found a way to hike within earshot or I could have known then that he wanted to hike alone. Perhaps I would have gone with him anyway. Or, I could have done something else with my life. At least by testing the partnership before we found ourselves stuck in the woods, we could have known what lay in store for each other. Maybe then we could have talked about our relationship and worked out whether we have enough in common to weather the difficulties that lay ahead. With my father there with us on Assateague, we would have had someone to guide us when we got off point or encourage us to dig deeper. At school, there were plenty of opportunities to discuss the trip — we lived one floor apart — but sometimes it takes leaving the day-to-day activities to get any real planning done.

We will never know.

As I walked from Maine to Connecticut, there was not a single day I was entirely alone. Human contact is not what I missed; I understand how one can feel lonely in New York City. We need more than a "Hi, how you doing" to feel connected. Connection requires a "Second Conversation" to dig deeper than the surface exchange of pleasantries like "Where you from?" "What you do?" or "How 'bout 'dem Iggles?" The conversation you need — to communicate —goes beyond the what, the where, the how, and who. It has to reach the why. "Why do we do the things we do." "Why do we want to do the things we have yet to do?" We guard these conversations tightly because once we play these cards, we have nothing left. But by not playing those cards, we fail to connect.

He left this morning to hitch to a larger town to buy a stove and to mail his tent home. We agreed to alternate the remaining food deliveries, although obviously he will get the food from his mother in Virginia and I will get the food from my Oak Ridge cousins. Without a tent, it will be lean-tos and tarps for me.

I also hitched a ride this morning, not to a bigger town, but to nearby Sharon, Connecticut, where I spent the day attending an open house at the Sharon Audubon Center. I attended lectures on edible plants, then sampled the food. I caught both the 11 AM workshop and then the same workshop at 1 PM. If they offered a 2 PM workshop, I would have attended that one too.

I could not get enough of milkweed sautéed in butter. Milkweed grows in marshy areas and ultimately forms a pod containing seeds that float in the wind on long white strands of silk, but while immature, sautéed in butter, it tastes like chicken.

Finding nothing else to eat, I hitched back to the Kent Congregationalist church which houses hikers in its basement. I did not want to go back the twenty-five miles to the Red Mountain Lean-to. Going back would mean that we would be hiking in close proximity. Tomorrow, I will leave Kent to begin a new journey — Alone.

AUGUST 3

Graymoor Monastery

It has been fun hiking alone. I still plan how far I wish to go each day but if I do not reach or do not like the destination I can sleep wherever I want. So far I have stayed exactly where I planned. And no one cares.

I met a Northbounder in Pawling, New York, who told me he also split with his partner. "In fact," he said, "with the exception of the Snail Sisters, I can't think of anyone who's still hiking with the same person."

I supposed that was meant to cheer me up, but whereas I passed three other Northbounders yesterday, who would keep him company, I was all alone. It seems the Northbounders hike together, fall back, advance ahead, and have a sense of community.

Although my partner and I spent very little time actually walking together, and did not talk much when we met for the nights, we did keep each other company when we visited towns. I was glad to have him as a partner when I fell sick in Maine. He suffered a fever in Massachusetts, and although he later complained I forced him to spend the night at the Mystery Lady's house, I am sure staying indoors in dry clothes helped his recovery more than spending the night in that dank, muddy hut. The biggest fear about hiking alone is getting sick or injured; at least someone else knows where you were last seen. Our relationship soured so much that, if one of us broke his leg, neither would have gone back to search. Once we reached that point, hiking alone added no more risk.

It rained all day, but I am dry now. After walking seventeen miles, I climbed the steep slope to the Graymoor Monastery. Although my Hollywood image of monasteries was darkness and mystery, Graymoor was legendary among Thruhikers as a warm and welcoming place that provided a good dinner and a dry bed. There is one other Thruhiker here, a Northbounder, who has fallen weeks off his pace due to a leg injury. If it takes him as long to hike to Katahdin as it has for me to reach here, he will be standing atop the Northern Terminus in snow. That is, unless the fires that now rage in Baxter State Park continue, in which case it will not be the cold that prevents him from climbing the "Towering Inferno." Hard to imagine that Maine now suffers a drought after the month I spent there.

He told me the Snail Sisters were all who remained behind him of the Northbounders and, no, he never heard of Pam Nelson. Reaching New York in August is late for a Northbounder hoping to climb Katahdin. I understand now why so many hike from south to north. If you leave Springer in March or April, the days get longer and the weather gets warmer. Because you cannot climb Katahdin too early in the spring, hiking south risks running out of light before reaching Georgia.

I have been hearing about the Snail Sisters for weeks and hope I will be on the Trail to meet them rather than ducking into an ice cream parlor. I would love to share a campsite with them; sit around a fire; maybe share a meal. They sound wonderful. Sometimes when I hike I try to imagine what they look like. I have long envisioned that night sharing a fire — not to mention the left handed zipper on my sleeping bag.

My room at the monastery has a single bed, a wood desk, and is lit by a bare light bulb, exactly what I expected. After stowing my gear, I went to the bathroom and took a shower, then used a pay phone to call home. My mother said that Mrs. Booz desperately wanted me to call her. Her son,

Mark, one of my housemates at school, lives in Allentown, Pennsylvania, and has my next food delivery.

I was due to meet Mark at the Allentown Lean-to eight days from now. The lean-to is just off Route 309, which crosses the AT due north of Mark's house. But Mrs. Booz explained that she has to attend a teachers' conference in State College and so asked if I could get there Monday, three days earlier. She said she had been planning the meals she was going to cook all summer and would be heartbroken if she could not do such a good deed, so could I come earlier — say, like, three days?

I looked at my map and told her to send Mark to meet me at the Delaware Water Gap by three PM on Monday the 8th. The Gap was a longer drive from Allentown but would be fifty-six miles this side of our original meeting place.

Later, as I sat at one of the tables, figuring out how I could hike the next 106 miles in four and a half days, a priest asked if he could join me. He introduced himself as Vince Blue and asked me about my experiences on the Trail. I told him a few tales, such as my brush up with the teenage moose.

Not surprisingly, the conversation turned to religion. He is a Jesuit who has studied the Judaic roots of Christianity. Besides Latin and Greek, he can read Hebrew and Aramaic — just one more Jesuit who astounded me by the depth of his learning and the breadth of his curiosity.

He knew a lot about Judaism at the time of Jesus. It was a time of great conflicts in the world, caused in part by the oppressive and evil empire of the Romans. The Jews were already an ancient people whose homeland bordered the eastern Mediterranean Sea, which turned out to be a bad location since that strip of land served as the main thoroughfare between the civilizations to the south and the north. Over time, invaders swept in from Assyria, Babylon, Greece, Rome, Arabia, Mongolia, and Turkey, slaughtering most of the Hebrew nation and sending the survivors into exile. After each wave of invader, the few remaining Jews came back to rebuild.

It was amidst the Roman conquest that Jesus was born, lived, and died — as a Jew. He was a teacher but his teachings were so anti-establishment, he became a threat to the Empire.

There is a saying: "I don't believe in organized religions; I'm a Jew." That was not always the case with Jews, as up to the time of Jesus, the religion had priests, a temple, and practices performed exclusively by the priests. Jesus, along with other rabbis, preached a direct connection with God that needed neither the physical structure of the Temple nor the intervention of a priestly class. Brother Blue said today's Rabbinic Judaism more resembles the religion Jesus espoused than it does the religion practiced in the Temple at the time of Jesus.

He told me that neither King Herod nor the high priest, Caiaphas, held any provenance to their positions and, in Herod's case, was not even Jewish. He may have been King of the Jews but he was not *of* the Jews. They were both Roman lackeys put into their positions to keep the Jews — and especially radicals like Jesus — in their place.

Although we were deep into this discussion, Brother Blue glanced at the time and abruptly excused himself for bed as he had an early mass to attend. That left me with much to ponder. Could the past two thousand years of religious wars, persecution, and intolerance all have been a big mistake?

AUGUST 6

The Last Northbounders

I left Graymoor with both my body and my soul nourished. The Trail continued down a steep slope through the parking lots and then turned west toward the Hudson River. As I walked with my massive blue pack, my brown beard, and my red hat, I suppose I was either a vision or a nightmare depending on one's perspective.

A thin woman with white hair and a slight stoop was walking up the steep slope toward the monastery. The perspective of the slope and my massive pack made me look like a giant to her. She asked me where I was heading and from where I had come. She never heard of the Appalachian Trail and could not understand why I would do such a thing. I explained a bit of the journey and compared it to the quest for the Holy Grail. She never heard of that either. I told her about the time I stood nose-to-nose with a moose; that impressed her. She was particularly interested in the mechanics of sending food to post offices along the way. With so many miles left to reach the Water Gap, she was taking up precious time, but I was as calm as a summer day, feeling especially saintly after my wonderful breakfast.

(If ever I start my own religion, I am going to proscribe the doctrine of eating a good breakfast.)

At last she said, "I better let you go." Then, just as I swung my pack onto my back, she said, "You'll remember to say a prayer for me?"

"Sure I will."

"You are Catholic, aren't you?"

I felt bad disappointing her. "No, I'm not."

"Protestant?"

"Not that either."

"Then —" with a look of fright awash on her face "what are you?"

"I'm Jewish."

"What? I — I ... Oh, I guess their prayers are good too."

Always good to feel like one of the boys.

The rain passed during the night and the sun greeted me in the parking lot as I said good bye. I felt rested and looked forward to crossing the rest of New York as quickly as possible. I walked over the Hudson River, using a bridge for a change. I passed a road crew taking a break from their resurfacing work. They took a keen interest in what I was doing although none said they would trade places. One pointed to my pack and asked, "Hey man, you got a piece in there?"

"Piece of what?" I asked.

"No man, a piece. Like — a rod."

"No, but my former hiking partner carries some fishing line and a few hooks. Why, once when we camped by this lake . . ."

"No man, not fish — I mean a gun."

"A gun? Why would I want to carry a gun? My pack is heavy enough."

"But what happens if you see a wild animal?"

"I watch it."

"Suppose it chases you?"

"I run."

Actually, after a discussion like that, wild animals were the least of my concern.

On the west side of the river, I entered the Bear Mountain State Park. Kids bussed from New York City stared at me as I walked through the park. One lad snuck behind and punched my pack. I told the group that assembled, "Hey, I don't mind — personally — if you sneak up behind me and hit my pack, but I can't be held responsible if so foolish an act triggers an explosion that could kill us all!"

From then on I walked under an escort of twenty to thirty kids forming a wide circle around me, lest I explode.

The climb to the top of Bear Mountain was steep but short and then the trail meandered to make sure it touched the rest of the park's mountains. Although the changes in elevation were not great, what made hiking in New York tiring was there were no ridges: it was either up or down.

I have two other complaints with New York. First, the occasional stretches of roads were guarded by vicious attack dogs. Whenever I walked down a road, I was compelled to carry a couple of rocks to fend off an attack. "That's okay, he won't bite," their owners would call as the huge creature would charge me with teeth bared.

"There's always a first time," I would reply, bouncing a rock off their brute's nose.

My other complaint is about the water — or lack of it. I carried water with me constantly and even then I ran dry before the next source. I cannot blame the entire state. I mean, it did try. Each day I passed another dry spring or stagnant creek. I recognized a waterfall by its moss covered rocks. The whole state was dry. I walked late into the night well after dark to reach what the guidebook called "a reliable spring." All my water bottles were empty and my throat was parched — oh, how I hate thirst worst of all — and I would need some water to make dinner. The water in the spring was still, warm to the touch, and smelled of rotten eggs. I boiled it then added orange drink mix to it. Then I put my container into the water to lower the temperature. When I tried it, the water tasted like warm, orange-flavored rotten eggs.

The next morning I walked to Richard's Hilltop Hideaway. This was another AT legend. Richard lives at the bottom of a ridge near the New York-New Jersey border. Each morning, he leaves thermoses of ice tea and the New York Times next to two beach chairs. I needed this ice tea badly as the sulfur-flavored orange juice was just not doing it for me. Unfortunately, according to the note left by the empty thermoses, Richard had left for the weekend. That meant no ice tea and no water for several more miles.

Nothing ventured, nothing gained. I followed the path down the ridge and found Richard's house where I filled the two empty thermoses with water from his garden hose and washed the pestilent orange sulfur juice out of my container, filling it with water for the dry day ahead.

Only in Bear Mountain Park did I have enough water. I needed to cover a lot of ground, especially after I dawdled through the historical display at the lodge. After descending from West Mountain, I turned onto a dirt trail along a small brook. Ahead of me, in the distance, I saw someone on a log. When I came closer, I could tell that the scrawny-legged fellow eating an over-stuffed corned beef special — fresh rye bread and red slices of corned beef with coleslaw and Thousand Island dressing — was no Thruhiker. He was as excited as a puppy, however, when I told him where I began.

Harold grew up on Staten Island reading and dreaming about the outdoors. That day, on his twenty-eighth birthday, he began his own quest. He planned to walk from the Hudson to the Delaware River, then canoe down the Delaware. I told him I was hiking to the Delaware River and that he could hike along with me. It worked: he gave me the other half of his sandwich.

Right away, I doubted whether Harold would make it. He lacked upper body strength, not to mention leg strength. I could see that he was going to hold me back. Still, he was someone to talk with; there could be no harm in letting him tag along for as long as he lasted. We walked a ways through a wood before coming upon a brook. When we reached the crossing, we waited for two women wearing baggy clothes and floppy hats to cross from the opposite side. One of them asked me, "Where did you hike from?" When I told her Katahdin, they both began asking me all sorts of questions. Then it hit me who they were.

"Oh my God! You're the Snail Sisters."

For the next twenty minutes we swapped stories like long lost friends. I told them about Charley, holed up with the Mystery Woman, which caused them to howl with laughter and relief to learn he made it to Massachusetts. They told me to make sure I try the whole wheat pizza at The Omega Health Food Store in the Delaware Water Gap. Meanwhile, poor Harold sat on a rock, not understanding why I was so happy to see two dirty, grubby women. God, I thought they were beautiful. All of a sudden, Harold became a nuisance, a third wheel crashing a party.

Although the bank of the brook would have made a lovely

place to camp, we all were several hours of hiking from the end of our day. How sad, but even when I meet people with whom I would love to share the night, I meet them at the wrong time. We said our goodbyes and I watched as they walked from view.

Several hours later, and not nearly as many miles as I would have liked, Harold and I ate dinner. I supplied the Long-Day Stew; he supplied the Devil Dogs. Nutrition was not Harold's strong point. The Trail had shaped my body and adjusted my biological clock. At five the next morning, I rolled up my sleeping bag for another day's hike. Harold stuck his head out of his sleeping bag and said, 'Wake me up at nine."

There lay my last chance to have a hiking partner. In the back of my mind I still hoped to meet Pam from the Appalachian Trail News, although that meeting would only be for dinner. I am kidding myself, actually; I know there would be no Northbounders behind the Snail Sisters.

I have come so far from Maine. I jumped into this journey without thinking. Following someone else's dream takes just as much work as following my own, and it can end just as badly. Unconsciously, I set myself up for a doomed partnership with my former friend; now I am alone. Partnerships dissolve and marriages fail — but have I learned anything, or, as Toynbee suggested, am I doomed to repeat it all again?

I swung on my pack, then looked down at Harold, exhausted from his one afternoon of hiking. Perhaps it was better this way. On to Springer Mountain. At that moment, though, something had changed. From then on, I knew, I would hike alone.

ACKNOWLEDGEMENTS

Thank you to:

J. MARK KLAMER for giving me my first chance to become a published author.

JOSEF BEERY for making this book beautiful and adding your unparalleled wisdom to the process of producing a book.

MONA ZAKHEIM who tore the first draft apart but encouraged me to go on.

BEN FELDMAN, a true Renaissance man, for setting such a high expectation and showing me how to reach it.

My wife **JULIA GRANT BAROL**, who understood and supported my need to get this book killed dead. I give you my love. Without your support and the granting of space, and your highly educated and critical eye for good literature, I could not have done it.

DR. RANDOLPH E. ELMQUIST, who gave me permission to use his name. Without you there would be no book. There are no bad guys here, just a pair of young men. Your focus and dedication are an inspiration. What's more, you finished the Trail and you lived your dream.

Note: all the names, places, and events actually happened. That is, with the exception of the name of the dog who accompanied us through the Mahoosics. His real name was Porky, but I changed it because I thought that would have sounded crude.

QUESTIONS AND TOPICS FOR DISCUSSION

This book explores several themes. Certainly one was the relationship between the partners. What were some of the others?

What are your feelings about the two main characters as persons? How would describe the evolution of these characters during the course of the journey?

Did they ever learn to communicate? How could they have made it better (remember, they had no cell phones let alone cell phone coverage)? Is this how you would have expected two young men to have handled their differences? What would you have advised them to do differently?

Do you believe it was the lack of calories that caused the physical and emotional strain? How would you have changed their menus?

What would you have done had you waited overnight for someone to show up?

Once they took the shortcut in Maine, would you consider them official "Thruhikers"? Where would you fall in the continuum of hikers he describes, between Steve Jackson at one extreme and Steve and Al (and Lance) on the other? Is skipping a section a matter of honor?

The storyteller paints multiple images of small rural towns. What were they? Which version dominates your image of rural America? Can you see yourself living alongside the Trail?

Why did the storyteller agree to hike with his friend? What would you have advised him if he were your friend or son?

If you were the storyteller, where in the story would you have ended the partnership – or would you?

He quotes, "A promise made is a debt unpaid." He also quotes, "A foolish consistency is the hobgoblin of little minds." Which of these describe his place on this trek?

Who was right about the fudge? Which social contract was violated?

The hiker said his father spent a summer working on a Vermont farm, far from home, then served in the Navy in both WWII and Korea. How did these experiences shape him? Was the Trail going to have a similar effect on these two young men?

Which is better parenting, protecting your children from the deprivation and near-death experiences described in the book or letting them do it?

The storyteller passes through a good chunk of America which makes him recall the community in which he grew up. Was his community typical of the one you grew up? How was it different? Which would you have preferred? What made his community survive?

This is a story whose two main characters were young men, however, there are women mentioned throughout the book. Is this an accurate portrayal of how young men see women? Were you surprised by his reaction when he finally met "The Snail Sisters"?

At the end of the book, when the main character sets off alone, do you think he is now more or less likely to reach Springer Mountain in Georgia?

ABOUT THE AUTHOR

David Barol is an acclaimed author, speaker, trainer, and financial consultant. His writing and speaking revolve around public policy and finance. He graduated from the University of Virginia, where he majored in Political and Social Thought, and then from Harvard University, where he holds a Masters in Public Policy from the Kennedy School.

Very active in his community, he lives near Philadelphia with his wife and three children. You can find his books at www.balahousepublishing.com or wherever great literature is sold.

LOGAN BREAD

A combination of different grains, honey, molasses, fat, and lead. It's the densest, driest substance known to man.

5 cups of water
4 pounds whole wheat flour
1 pound soy flour
1 1/2 cups blackstrap molasses
1 1/2 cups honey
2 1/2 cups dark brown sugar
1/4 teaspoons baking powder
1 cup melted shortening

1 ounce lead (optional)

Stir ingredients together then bake in a two inch deep pan for one hour at 350°. Cut into squares then leave to dry in a partially open warm oven for twelve hours. Serve with peanut butter.

Made in the USA
Middletown, DE
06 May 2016